ABUNDANCE OF
JOY

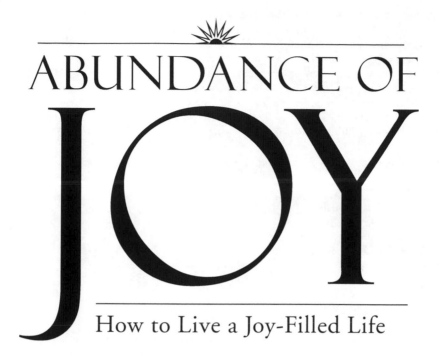

ABUNDANCE OF JOY

How to Live a Joy-Filled Life

HELEN MARTINO-BAILEY

BALBOA.
PRESS
A DIVISION OF HAY HOUSE

Artwork by BirdBrain Logic, Nik Carson

Balboa Press books may be ordered through booksellers or by contacting:

Balboa Press
A Division of Hay House
1663 Liberty Drive
Bloomington, IN 47403
www.balboapress.com.au
1-(877) 407-4847

ISBN: 978-1-4525-0700-2 (sc)
ISBN: 978-1-4525-0701-9 (e)

Printed in the United States of America

Balboa Press rev. date: 06/12/2013

CONTENTS

Preface xi
Introduction... xiii
Before we Begin, Some Key Points of My Philosophy xvii

Part I
Learning the Art of Joy

Chapter 1: Creating New Understandings 3
Chapter 2: Unlocking Joy 14
Chapter 3: Spotting Joy 22
Chapter 4: Taking Action.. 25
Chapter 5: Feeling Joy 30
Chapter 6: Appreciating Joy 36
Chapter 7: The Joy of Peace 44
Chapter 8: The Heart of Joy 52

Part II
Understanding the Things that Bring You Joy

Chapter 9: Creating Your List of Joys 61
Chapter 10: Developing Your List of Inner Joys 70

Part III
The Four Tools and Four Factors
that Lead to a Joy-Filled Life

Chapter 11: The Four Tools 83
Chapter 12: Using Tool Four Effectively.......................... 98

Chapter 13: The Four Factors 107
Chapter 14: Applying the Four Factors 118

Part IV
More Tips to Living Life with Joy

Chapter 15: Helpful Questions to Ask when the
            Going Gets Tough 129
Chapter 16: The Medicinal Powers of Joy 138
Chapter 17: Joy at Work 148
Chapter 18: Holding on to Joy 160
Chapter 19: Getting Rid of Negative Energy 168
Chapter 20: Quick Fixes 176
Chapter 21: Embracing Joy 184

Part V
Bringing It All Together with the Daily Checklists

Chapter 22: How to Start Your Day with Joy 191
Chapter 23: How to Live Your Day with Joy 200
Chapter 24: How to End Your Day with Joy 207

This book is dedicated to you

It is written in the loving memory of Angela Anastas
whose courage and love of life inspired all who knew her.

In writing this book I give thanks to:

My unending source of love—*Divine Energy*.

My husband who lovingly supports me through
every step of my journey. You are my love.

Sally Webster and Michael Wheatley for their proof
reading skills. What amazing eyes you both have!

All my family and friends. You bring me joy. I love you all.

PREFACE

I work with people from all walks of life, helping them to better manage their personal circumstances. The life-challenges they present with are varied—health issues, relationship troubles, financial woes, family dramas, dealing with the loss of a loved one, facing an impending court action. For whatever reason they are drawn to me one thing is common to all: life for them holds little joy.

Yet, in spite of their challenging problems, right from our very first session I enable them to experience feelings that include joy. This occurs because I take them on an inner-journey—to a place within that houses precious jewels. And every time they are touched by one of these priceless gems they feel *joy.*

In truth, I do nothing magical for them other than acquaint them with the repository of the jewels—with the source of joy that lives within them every second of the day—their spirit.

We cannot find real joy until we live through the joy that belongs to our spirit.

INTRODUCTION

I have written this book with one goal in mind, and that is to help you experience more joy in your life.

I adore joy. Just the word alone fills me with excitement. Joy has many transformational qualities, and life becomes richer, happier, fuller, lighter, less stressful and more manageable when we live it with joy.

Anyone can improve his or her life through joy, and I am going to teach you *how* this is possible. Yes, *how* . . . and in practical ways that you can apply to your life right now!

There's more to joy than feeling good and being happy and in reading this book, you will learn to understand the energy of joy more fully. Joy is the extension of who we are. It is the energy, the vibrancy that lives in the centre of your heart.

To help you experience this, I have provided you with an extensive array of tips, tools, exercises and suggestions that will help you to do the following:

- Enjoy life more.
- Create helpful habits.
- Improve the way you think and feel.
- Make better life choices.
- Lessen ego control.
- Improve your health.
- Bring a spark to your day.

All these changes and more occur when we deliberately choose to live life with joy.

Throughout the book I share with you some of the information that I teach in my workshops and personal sessions. Like my first book, *Journey of our Spirit*, each chapter begins and ends with messages that I have received from *Spirit*. (Since 1993, through the process of automatic writing, I have received messages—words of wisdom—from the White Brotherhood and various spirit teachers. For ease of reading I collectively name my higher teachers "Spirit"). I have chosen to keep this format because many readers have asked for more of *Spirits'* inspiring messages, and secondly, the exercises, tools and factors within this book are a direct result of applying *Spirits'* messages—in practical ways—to my life. I want to share with you how I have achieved this and how their inspiring words can help you too.

To get the best out of this book I recommend that you try all of the different exercises given, especially the exercise in Chapter 9: Creating Your List of Joys. You may choose to read the book through once and then return to this exercise so that you can complete it more thoroughly. That's fine. This particular exercise is important because it is essential for the four tools and four factors, which, as you will soon discover, are *key ingredients* that can transform your life.

To make it easier for you to complete some of the exercises in the book you can go to my website www.lightwords.com.au and download the appropriate information sheets.

View this book as a life-enhancing manual. Keep it handy and return to it for guidance and inspiration. Let it help motivate and uplift you into joyfulness.

It brings me great joy to share my book with you. Through it may you come to know, feel and experience the abundance of joy that lives within you!

Helen

BEFORE WE BEGIN, SOME KEY POINTS OF MY PHILOSOPHY . . .

Life

Life is a creating, conscious energy.

We are not separate from the energy of life. We live within it and it (the energy of life) lives within us.

We communicate to the energy of life through the energy vibrations of our thoughts and feelings.

By improving our thoughts and feelings we can improve our life experience.

We have both the power and the choice to change how we think and feel.

Our Spirit

We consist of a body, mind and spirit (spirit-self).

Our spirit-self has a consciousness and the consciousness of our spirit-self goes beyond personality, ego, mind and emotions. It communicates information to us through intuitive thoughts and inner-feelings.

Our spirit-self is a knowledgeable resource that can help us to live a better life.

When we ignore the higher knowledge of our spirit-self we limit our full potential.

Joy

Joy is more than an emotion. It is a core feeling that originates from our spirit-self.

We desire joy because joy is the nature of who we are.

PART I

LEARNING THE ART OF JOY

*When you find joy in what you are doing,
it is easier to enjoy what you do!*

CHAPTER 1

CREATING NEW UNDERSTANDINGS

*"Joy is a sound investment that
delivers great returns."*

—*Words from Spirit*

Life can be viewed as an investment.

Each day we invest our time and energy in making deposits and withdrawals into our 'life' savings account. Joy, love and laughter are examples of energy deposits that credit our personal account; they make us feel good, and they improve our life experience. Guilt, blame and stress are examples that draw down on our account; they lessen our enjoyment of life.

The personal energy investments (PEIs) that we choose to transact each day are vitally important because these investments are the ones that return to us a healthy (or not-so-healthy) state of wellbeing; these are the ones that determine how much pleasure we get from life.

This book aims to teach you how to enhance your PEIs through engaging joy. Becoming more conscious of your daily PEIs and using joy as a tool to improve them is one of the best measures you can take to increase your investment portfolio!

Before you progress to the many joy-enhancing techniques and derive the most from them, there are a few understandings that I need to bring to light.

The Truth about Joy

Joy is a great feeling that is very beneficial to our lives. It has many positive effects on our health and wellbeing. However, not many of us live each day with joy! Why?

Most of us *wait* for joy to happen in our lives. We wait for good times to occur, for our lives to improve, for happy occasions to manifest, for hard times to change, for relationships to blossom. We wait until life conditions are good, and *then* we feel joy.

This is not a very effective method, for a lot of time can be wasted in waiting for the right circumstances to appear in our lives.

There is a better way, one that involves less waiting and more creating! This technique, which you are about to learn, provides greater opportunities for joy to flow through your life daily. It differs from the norm because it takes a holistic approach to joy and because it teaches you how to channel your personal energies in the right way. In applying this method you will see that life conditions *don't have to be exactly as you want them to be in order for you to experience joy.*

Fabulous!

Sourcing Joy

Most of us have learned that joy is a delightful physical emotion found in satisfying experiences, material items, great relationships and happy thoughts. These sources—which bring pleasure to the *body and mind*—are wellsprings for joyful feelings.

To increase our ability to experience more joy throughout life, we need to expand our options. A key point that helps expand our ability to experience joy is in the understanding of where joy originates. Identifying the point of origin of joy means we become privy to a source that is rich in joyful feelings.

Where Joy Begins

Contrary to what we may think, joy does not begin as an emotion. Our emotions are lifted *as a result of feeling joy,* but the source from where joy springs is deep *within.*

Our spirit—our spirit-self—is the birthplace, the abode, and the point of origin of joy. *It's* the source, the *feeling* from where joy blooms.

This understanding is quite different from the norm. Most understand joy as a physical emotion (as opposed to a feeling) that delights the body and mind. But if we understand joy purely as a physical emotion our potential to experience joy becomes limited.

When we understand that joy is the fabric and the very nature of our spirit-self, and that we have the ability to tap into this rich source of joy, we harness our full potential.

Being able to access joy of our spirit-self is what takes our experience of joy to a whole new level. It's the cornerstone to experiencing greater joy throughout our lives.

Our Spirit-Self has Value

To try and understand the nature of joy without including our spirit-self in the equation is a mistake, for it means that we miss out on a whole load of fabulous feelings that deeply enrich our lives, feelings that have the potential to sustain us in joy for long periods of time.

Our spirit-self has many life skills to offer. In fact, when it comes to joy, it has an abundance of skills to offer, and the good news is that learning to access the joy within our spirit-self is easy. It's my area of expertise, and I will show you how to tap into this amazing resource. Excellent!

So our approach to joy will be all-inclusive. All aspects of our being—body, mind *and spirit*—have a role to play when it comes to joy, and all aspects are important.

Relating to Life

Along with our holistic approach we will also take into account how *we relate* to the energy of life through our PEIs and how the energy of life *responds* to our daily PEIs. There's a lot going on that we don't see.

The Energy of Life

Every moment of the day, the cells of our body respond to how we think, what we feel, how we act and what we do. Our cells are constantly sensing and feeling the energy we hold.

Every moment of the day, the energy of life responds to how we think, what we feel, how we act and what we do. Life is constantly sensing and feeling our presence within its energy.

We are not separate from life, and neither are we separate from our thoughts, our feelings or our cells! All affect one, and one affects all.

The Law

There are some simple laws of life that, when embraced, improve our experiences tremendously because they take into account the inseparable interaction that we have with the energy of life. Many of you may know these laws as the laws of attraction or energy attraction. Whilst this is not a book about the law of attraction per se, I do want to highlight a key concept of energy attraction that is pertinent to joy, and that is the law of magnetic attraction.

Like everything within life, the thoughts and feelings that we hold can simply be broken down to forms of energy. As forms of energy they draw to them, like a magnet, energy of similar kinds, vibrations that are either positive or negative.

The energy that you project onto life *through your thoughts and feelings* is matched and drawn back to you. What you think and feel each moment of the day attracts and creates more of the same vibrations to your life; like attracts like.

Taking this law in relation to joy, if you believe that you are lacking joy, and you are in the habit of reinforcing these types of thoughts, then you'll experience an absence of joy in your life. This is because your PEIs—in the form of your thoughts and feelings—are magnetically drawing to you a carbon copy of what you are projecting. Life mirrors what you tell it. If your personal vibrations send messages out to the energy of life that say, "I lack joy," the resultant *energy pattern* that you draw and attract to your life is a "lack of joy."

If this is what is happening in your life right now there are ways to change this for yourself, break the pattern that you are creating, and improve your experiences.

There are ways to direct your thoughts and feelings so that you work effectively with the energy of life, and as a result of doing so, create better outcomes for yourself.

Focus of Attention

One way to do this is to become more conscious of your focus of attention—that is, become more deliberate about ensuring that your *focus of attention is heavily weighted towards the feelings of joy*. This is a great step that will help you to create more joy, and you'll learn how to do this.

You may think, "There are many circumstances happening in my life right now that aren't joyful," or perhaps there are circumstances from your past and their effects still trouble you. How is it possible for you to think and feel joy when life's difficult? Whilst it is not possible to be full of joy all of the time, there are strategies that you can employ that will help you feel better during difficult times and return you to more positive feelings as soon as practical. Excellent!

The focus of the strategies that you are about to learn centre on working with the energy of life in positive ways. They aim to improve your PEIs so that even during difficult times you are able to continue to attract joy to you. And the joy you attract will help lift you during the challenging life circumstances.

The Two Top Joy Enhancers

Incorporating the skills of our spirit-self and the laws of energy attraction into our understanding and application of joy are key elements because (1) the virtues of our *spirit-self* teach us how to *live life* in higher ways and (2) the *law of attraction* teaches us how to *work with life* in higher ways.

Applied together, like two hands, they are more helpful and more efficient than one. They form a magical combination that rapidly increases our ability to experience joy.

So our approach to joy will be all-encompassing. It involves improving our PEIs so that we get the best out of our body, mind and spirit and the best from the energy of life.

In order to do this, here are some points worthy of consideration.

Joy—Decide How Often You Want It

It's good to have goals in life as goals give us direction and focus. With regard to joy, it's helpful to have a clear idea in your mind of just how often you want to experience joy. Are you happy to continue experiencing joy intermittently from time to time, or would you prefer a daily dose?

My recommendation is to set your sights high. Approach life with the attitude: "I love joy, and I want to experience it daily!" Why not aim high and make this your personal goal? Joy is free. It is always available to you. You may not believe how that is possible right now; however, it is, and your life will improve immeasurably through joy.

The Truth

Like any new skill that we undertake, we have to work at it, and joy is no exception. Initially, it takes work because you are changing ingrained habits that you have grown up with, habits that are not helpful in assisting you to experience joy. Although it takes concentration and effort, once you incorporate some of the practices into your life, it becomes much easier.

Here are three qualities that will assist you in mastering joy. I call them the essential three P's: practice, persistence, and patience.

Practise the exercises contained within this book. They are specifically designed to increase your daily experiences of joy. Also, they bring out your best side.

Persistence pays off. Getting rid of old habits is not a quick fix (darn!). Performing the practices once or twice (or here and there) won't change ingrained behaviours. You need to hold firm and remain committed to your purpose of self-improvement through joy. Persist, and you *will* succeed.

Patience is what will take you there. It's an essential attribute that will ensure you are triumphant.

Take Charge

Whilst it's good to go with the flow of life, when it comes to joy, action is required. This involves putting yourself into the driver's seat—of life—and steering your travels so that you set a course towards joy.

Inevitably, life circumstances will cause you to detour from joy at times, but like all detours, see them as *temporary inconveniences that you can drive around*. And when it's appropriate, get yourself back on course, headed towards your daily destination of joy.

Living with joy won't mean that from now on everything in your life is going to be all bright and happy. Life will still present challenges; it has to for our personal development and spiritual growth. We have to live out the ups and downs of our 'life contract.' However, joy will help you to develop better *life-management skills* that will get you through life's twists and turns and help you overcome life's difficulties.

Joy is a sound investment that pays good dividends in good times and bad, but success in mastering joy can only be reached when you take charge, set your sights, and take personal responsibility for joy in your life. Unless you do these things, reaching your goal will be difficult.

We're Starting Anew

You are about to learn a completely new approach to joy. In order to make the most of the information that will be presented to you, here are some pointers. You'll find the forthcoming exercises more effective if you are prepared to do the following:

- Be open to seeing things a little differently.
- Be willing to value all aspects of your being—body, mind and spirit.
- Give the suggestions a go. They can't hurt you!
- Do a little personal work.

Warming Up to Our Approach

In order to get things moving along, we're going to begin with eight warm-up exercises. These techniques begin the process of broadening our vision and approach to joy. They are designed to get joy flowing.

So, let's not waste any more time. Let's get into joy because . . . joy is in you!

Keys to the Abundance

- You greatly improve your life experience when you invest in joy.
- Your ability to experience joy increases when you approach joy in a holistic way—body, mind and spirit.
- It's necessary to take charge, and start driving your life towards joy!

"Let us not forget that each day is a gift. If we treat each day with joy and reverence we have not wasted time."

—Words from Spirit

CHAPTER 2

UNLOCKING JOY

*"Be not afraid to unlock the greatest joy
within you, the joy of your spirit."*

—Words from Spirit

Believe it or not, we all hold notions about joy. For instance, we may believe that we can only feel joy when we are happy, that certain circumstances need to occur in order for us to feel joy, that we are undeserving of joy, or that we lack a lot of things that could bring us joy.

We may regurgitate thoughts that prevent joy from entering our life—thoughts that stem from personal belief systems that make us afraid to feel joy.

Conditioning, past pains and fears all colour our impressions of joy.

And if all these things are not enough to contend with we hold certain habits that block joy. Perfectionism, selfishness and laziness are examples of character traits that can quell joy, as can emotional reactions such anger, blame and silence. Any of these habitual reactions can block joy, and if we are not careful we can turn "not feeling joyful" into a habit!

In order to develop healthier beliefs and habits we are going to engage in a system upgrade. The suggestions and visualisations in the chapters ahead are focused on new ways to improve your understanding of joy. They will help you to see joy differently and these new insights will bring many benefits to your life.

The best way to approach these insights is firstly to view them as innovative ways that are designed to enhance your skills in joy. *Joy is a skill*, and upgrading your proficiency is an essential step in mastering joy.

Secondly, see the process that you are about to engage in as being similar to what happens when you are installing new computer software. New software overrides old programming, and in effect, this is what we'll be doing—upgrading our old operating systems by improving upon our current beliefs and habits. Like all new software it may take some getting used to, but it will have you running your life more effectively and joyfully.

The more you embrace and apply the strategies given, the more skilled you become at mastering joy.

If, while you are engaging in the strategies, old thoughts surface that undermine your new beliefs you can thwart them by telling yourself, "I am in the process of engaging in a system upgrade!" How good is that!

First, Let's Imagine!

Current research in the science of neuroplasticity, in relation to brain pathways, reveals that each time we learn or experience something new, our brain is rewired. New connections are made and old ones wither away.

One powerful way of rewiring and supporting new information in our brain is through the technique of visualisation—that is, creating pictures in our mind that purposefully create positive outcomes. Top athletes use this technique as a way to improve their performances. To improve our understandings of joy we will engage in some imagery techniques.

Creating Form

Let's begin with an exercise that assists our mind to appreciate that joy can be found within.

Previously I mentioned that joy originates from our spirit-self. For many, this is not only a new concept to grasp but a difficult one to conceptualise because our spirit-self doesn't have form or identity, and our mind finds it hard to relate to something that is without form.

To overcome this barrier it's helpful to generate an image that *represents our spirit-self as being a source of joy*. And we need to do this early in the piece so that throughout the book you can recall this symbolic image to mind—ideally, each time the words *spirit-self, joy* and *inner joy* are mentioned.

When we create a mental picture that denotes inner joy and the richness this joy holds, then our mind is put at ease. From then on the mind has a reference point, an image that it can relate to and draw on.

Now a curious thing about our mind is if we create an image that is a little different—a little fanciful as opposed to actual—we are more likely to remember the image because it leaves a greater impression. Therefore, the picture that I'm going to give you may seem a little offbeat, but I will explain my reasons for giving you this image later in the chapter.

So in order to help our mind get used to the idea that our spirit-self is a source of inner joy, here is a little exercise.

Warm-Up Exercise #1: Unlocking the Spirit of Joy within You

From now on, when you think of your spirit-self and the bounty of *inner joy that it holds, imagine it* in this light:

> *Visualise a treasure chest.* A bountiful treasure chest, one that is open, full, *self-replenishing* and truly magnificent! The treasure chest you imagine may contain an abundance of precious jewels; it may house an array of amazing colours, bars of gold, endless dollars or mixed gems.
>
> It's your treasure chest. Therefore, you should fill it and picture it as creatively as you like.
>
> Now imagine this treasure chest as being within you. See it situated right in the middle of your chest in close proximity to your heart. This is its home; it's where your treasure chest lives and resides.
>
> And it's located there so that its jewels lift you; its gems have the power to raise your heart.

So to help your mind conceptualise your spirit and its role with regard to joy, liken your spirit-self to a bountiful treasure chest that is filled with inner riches that lift your heart in joy.

Let Go!

The imagery that I am asking you to create is not one to get bogged down with or be too analytical about. It works best if you can let go and allow your mind to explore the imagery and the ideas.

When it comes to experiencing joy, your spirit-self is part of the equation. It's not all of the equation, but it is a *very important part*. Being open to the idea that your spirit-self can bring a wealth of joy to your life is helpful. So don't worry too much about the how's and why's at this stage. Instead, have fun creating your treasure chest within.

If you're finding it hard to mentally capture the image then why not take a moment to look at pictures of treasure chests? You can easily find examples online. This will help you create your own personal image.

Also it's helpful to recognise that the visualisation of the treasure chest is simply a metaphor for your spirit-self—an analogy. Understanding the imagery in this light makes it easier for the mind to accept and create the image.

Enhance the Effects

Here are two ideas you might try that enhance the effects of the imagery: Firstly, foster good feelings as you imagine. It feels great to think about the possibility of such wealth existing within our heart, doesn't it? Therefore support the imagery by *feeling good* about the treasure chest and the bounty it holds.

To really rev up the good feelings, I often place my hands on my chest and take a brief moment to visualise my treasure chest within. Then I spend time focusing on all of the good feelings that surface and bubble up inside of me. It feels great just to take a few seconds to soak up the inner feelings that spontaneously emerge when I think of my inner treasure chest.

The second suggestion is to *affirm positive thoughts* that support the imagery. For example, when I'm imagining my treasure chest, I often repeat in my mind, "My spirit-self is a treasure. Its riches fill me with joy!" I recite these words as I imagine. This supports the imagery and generates even more good feelings.

Why Visualise a Treasure Chest?

Firstly, it helps our mind open up to the idea that our spirit-self is a rich resource. We don't often appreciate our spirit-self in this light. So by choosing an image that symbolises great wealth, our mind begins to place value on our spirit.

This action also reinforces the fact that our spirit-self is the *holder* of many priceless jewels. As you will come to see, these jewels are the qualities within you, the values that you have and you hold.

You'll come to know these qualities soon, and you'll learn how to access them; however, for now, keep envisioning your beautiful, bountiful, self-replenishing treasure chest. Be playful in your imaginings and, most importantly, feel good that a treasure exists within you. It does. It truly does!

Okay, let's move on to the next reinforcing exercise.

Warm-Up Exercise #2: The Centre of Joy

In the middle of the word "joy" is the letter "o." Place your attention on this letter and allow the letter to remind you that the centre of "joy" lives within "you."

Use this image to support and reinforce the previous one. When you see the "o" in the word joy, let it prompt you to briefly re-imagine and remind you of your treasure chest within.

When you associate the two images together you strengthen the frequency and the impact of the imagery on your mind.

Excellent! These two exercises will help create new brain pathways that retrain your mind to do the following:

- See your spirit-self in a new light.
- Develop recognition that your spirit-self is a rich source of joy.
- Develop the concept that there's a source of joy to be found within.

Now that's a broader view of joy for your mind to enjoy!

I recommend that you engage in the suggested imagery often, for this exercise helps bring to light that your spirit-self is a repository of joy.

Keys to the Abundance

- Imagine a bountiful treasure chest residing in the middle of your chest. See it as a rich source of joy that has the power to raise your heart.
- Feel good that this wealth of joy lives within your heart.
- Whilst visualising your treasure chest affirm, "My spirit-self is a treasure. Its riches fill me with joy!"

"Believe in the magic of joy. Joy has the power
to transform your life. Believe this to be so."

—*Words from Spirit*

CHAPTER 3

SPOTTING JOY

*"Are your eyes looking for joy, or are
they closed to the joys of life?"*

—Words from Spirit

When it comes to seeing the joys in our life, we're not very skilled. Too many times our eyes are focused on our personal problems, often blaming others for the lack of joy that we feel. The truth is, other people *play a part* in our joyful experiences, but it's not up to others to make us feel joyful. Living life with joy is our own responsibility!

Here is an empowering exercise that trains our brains to focus on the many joys that occur each day. For life holds many joys and it's uplifting to see them.

Warm-Up Exercise #3: Joy Spotting

From now on you have a mission. Each day, your aim is to witness at least *one* passing scene that delights your heart. To do this, look around you in all the many environments that you find yourself in throughout the day and spot a scene that uplifts you. (It's as if you're a photographer that's in search of capturing the prized snapshot of the day!).

Your search may lead you to witness a glorious scene of nature; kindness between people; the specialness in a stranger's smile; the beauty of the human condition; a funny moment. Each day look for and capture a snapshot of life that lifts your heart. Once you have found it instil the image to mind so that when you recall it later on, you experience good feelings.

Some days you may be privy to many joyful scenes (terrific!). If this is the case, at the end of the day, choose one scene from the many, the one that's extra special.

The purpose of this practice is to train your mind to look for joy daily. If you include more joyful scenes in the environment that you witness each day, your brain learns to "see" more joy in your life. Also, this practice helps to *attract* more joyful scenes to your life. How?

The process is similar to what happens to a woman when she's pregnant. Before pregnancy, she hardly notices other pregnant women, but once she is pregnant, her attention changes. Because she is thinking about pregnancy, the change in mental focus causes her to see pregnant women, notice them more often and attract them to the different environments that she encounters.

As previously mentioned, one of the governing laws of life is that you attract to your life more of what your focus and attention is on. If your attention is on seeing joy, then you'll witness and attract more joy to your life!

Make *joy-spotting* your new *daily habit!* Indulge your sight and fill your senses and spot the joy in your day. And in the evening before you retire to bed, recall your special snapshot. Use the image to help your mind focus on a positive scene before you fall sleep.

Keys to the Abundance

- Each day, go joy-spotting. Find the prize winning snapshot of the day, and regularly recall this scene to mind.
- Enjoy the good feelings that surface when you mentally recollect the scene.
- Recall the scene to mind before going to sleep.

*"Within every day lies a gift. It may be small,
it may be well packaged, it may be difficult to
find—but no day ever passes without something
special occurring. Look for the gift in each day
and be grateful for its presence in your life."*

—*Words from Spirit*

CHAPTER 4

TAKING ACTION

*"If you make joy your destination, then peace
and love will accompany you on your journey."*

—*Words from Spirit*

In learning new skills, our greatest stumbling block is often putting the new skills into action. To successfully master joy, it's important that we take action.

A step that makes it easier to take action is to be clear about the direction that you want to take. When you are clear about where you are heading, engaging in action becomes easier.

Think of it in this light: Once you *know* the destination for your next holiday vacation, it's easier to take action (make arrangements) that will help you get there. We can apply the same thinking processes that are involved in holiday planning to joy.

We can make joy our destination (our inner journey), a personal goal and objective that we wish to direct and head towards *daily*. How can we reach this goal?

Firstly, as you do when you are planning a holiday, *feel positive and excited* about your (inner) journey and keep your thoughts on your destination (joy). Then support your goal with this affirmative statement: *"Joy is important to me."* Say this several times. Write the affirmation on some Post-it notes and place them within your environment.

After some time you won't need the reminder notes, but to begin with you need to make it clear to your mind that joy is important to you—it's something that you want to experience daily and it's something that you value.

Now this exercise will help make it happen.

Warm-Up Exercise #4: Taking Action Today

This is a self-care and self-awareness exercise that involves learning to engage in the simple things each day, for the simple things in life are great joy-boosters. They are food for your soul.

There are many joy-enhancing activities that you can do daily that won't cost you money, activities that don't involve buying things, getting intoxicated, sexual gratification, gambling or relying on other people to give you joyful satisfaction.

Here are a few suggestions of activities that may get your joy juices flowing:

- Listen to your favourite music
- Watch a funny movie or video clip on the internet
- Hug your partner, your children or a friend
- Walk the dog
- Dance
- Sing along to your favourite song/s

- Take a bubble bath
- Be spontaneous
- Perform a random act of kindness
- Complete a task that you have had on hold. (Completing the task will make you feel better)
- Unclutter your desk/wardrobe/pantry/workshop. (Again, the act of doing and completing the task will make you feel great)
- Exercise to music
- Do a creative activity, such as drawing, sketching, cooking, composing or creating something
- Spend time at the beach or the park
- Volunteer your time to help someone
- Plant vegetables in your garden

The idea is to engage in an activity that is easy to do, one that doesn't cost money yet lifts your heart.

We often make excuses as to why we can't do an activity. We tell ourselves: "I'm too busy right now;" "I'll leave this activity for another day;" "I'll do this when I am feeling better about myself;" "I'll do this when I finish reading the book." Learn to take charge and do it *now*.

If you happen to be reading this book at bedtime, then make the commitment to follow through on this activity first thing in the morning.

Once you have carried out your action make a brief notation about the activity. (For example, "I danced for five minutes"). Then put the note where you can see it during the day, and in the early evening place the note on top of your pillow or somewhere where you will read it before you retire to bed.

Revising the activity is an act of reinforcement. It reminds you that today you took a step towards joy and that you invested some of your personal energy in joy because *joy is important to you!*

Excellent!

The end of inaction begins with taking action. Simple joys are an easy way of taking effective action, and they're a great way to keep you feeling good each day.

Keys to the Abundance

- Each day review your life goal and destination, namely joy.
- Throughout the day affirm the statement, "Joy is important to me."
- Take a moment each day to engage in a simple action that delivers joy.

"Cherish the simple things in life. Cherish the blessings and joys that surround you each day—your family and friends; the beauty of nature; the many experiences that colour your life in a positive way. Many search for more things to make them happy but it is the simple things that add great joy to living. Be aware of them. Enjoy and appreciate life's blessings."

—Words from Spirit

CHAPTER 5

FEELING JOY

*"Feel love, think love; feel joy, think joy. Feel
peace, think peace. When you live this way
you experience life through your spirit."*

—*Words from Spirit*

In order to fully embrace Warm-Up Exercise #5 some
background information is necessary, namely the effects of
joy on your wellbeing.

We know joy to be a positive, powerful feeling that makes us
feel good. We also know that certain experiences, such as
worrying thoughts, stresses, unresolved matters of the heart,
physical ailments, anger and tiredness can make us feel *not so
good*. Any one of these lessens our sense of joy.

What we *feel* tells us a lot, and it is a key point in relation to
joy. Often we try to attain joy by improving our thoughts but
do nothing about improving our feelings. Joy ultimately is a
feeling, not a thought. Thoughts can bring on the feelings of
joy, but we experience joy as something that's felt within our
bodies.

When we engage in joy-spotting, for instance, as we witness the special moment, we are touched by feelings, feelings that spring from within. These feelings make us feel good. They lift our thoughts and mood.

The key to mastering joy is to pay more attention to improving our feelings. Lifting our feelings first makes it easier for our thoughts to follow suit and improve.

Getting to Know the Real Feeling of Joy

Joy houses an expansive array of feelings. It's greater than the positive emotions that we normally equate it with, namely happiness and pleasure. These positive emotions are expressions of a joyful state. They are not the sum total of joy.

Housed deep within your being, joy exudes qualities like peace, calmness, contentment, vibrancy, excitement and fun. It arouses many feelings and your treasure chest is filled with these delightful feelings, which we'll soon explore.

As well as holding qualities, joy has an energy vibe to it. *We feel this vibration within our bodies.* When you are full of joy, there is a buzz within you, a vibe that feels good. For instance, when you think of something that brings you joy, wow, your body gets a bit tingly and excited. When you earnestly affirm, "Joy is important to me," there is a resonance, a rhythm, a pulsation and an excitement within your body that tells you, "Yep, this belief feels good to me. It feels great!"

The feeling of joy holds a strong positive vibration. It's more than a happy and pleasurable emotion. *It's an energy felt within the body.*

It Helps to Be Clear—Are You Experiencing a Feeling or an Emotion?

Often in our thoughts and expressions the two words *feelings* and *emotions* are used interchangeably, but they are not exactly the same. There are subtle differences, and in the context of experiencing joy, it's important to understand the differences.

Feelings present themselves in two ways. We have physical feelings that belong to our body—hunger, pain and thirst are some examples. Then there are sensory feelings or *inner feelings* within our body. For example, the feeling of general wellbeing, or the feeling of vibrancy as we dance or sing. Inner feelings do not have emotional content. They're simply the *sensation* of what's going on inside us.

Emotions are slightly different from feelings. They are *reactions,* responses to the sensations we are feeling. We may have the physical feeling of pain in our body, and we could react to the pain by getting angry. We *charge the feeling that we are experiencing with an emotion*. Here's another example: We may have the inner feeling of feeling fit, but then someone makes a comment that is disparaging towards our physique. Our response to their comment could stir hurtful emotions or light-hearted ones (we could laugh off the comment). Either way, we choose the reaction to the comment made. *We choose what emotions to apply to our feelings.*

Feelings are not "heady" like emotions. They don't lie. They don't tell us stories. They just simply "are" *sensing what is, what feels right, and what does not feel right*. They *sense* and *receive* information within our bodies, and they tell us if what we are experiencing feels good or not so good.

There are subtle shades of differences between feelings and emotions. You will come to discover how to read the shades of differences.

The Most Beneficial Feelings

The most powerful inner feelings that we house are the ones that belong to our spirit-self. I previously gave examples of some of the inner feelings that belong to our spirit-self: peace, calmness, contentment, vibrancy, excitement and fun. These feelings are innate. They are always within us but, more often than not, they are being crushed by emotional baggage.

If I got you to lie down during a bout of anger and then proceeded to play relaxing music for you, this music would likely relax you, allowing peaceful feelings to surface.

Whilst you were angry the feeling of peace—which is an innate feeling within you—did not up and leave your body. What happened was your conscious attention of it was diverted for a while. *Covered over* by emotional baggage your *awareness of its presence* shifted. Once the emotion of anger was lifted you were then able to feel peaceful feelings again.

The inner feelings that belong to our spirit-self are the most powerful of all feelings. They are the *definitive feelings that tell us if we are in harmony with our body, mind and spirit*. They are the jewels within our treasure chests.

Through engaging in the positive feelings of our spirit-self we increase our daily experiences of joy. Soon these inner feelings will be brought to your attention so that you can use them to your advantage. Fabulous!

Warm-Up Exercise #5: Opening Your Ability to Feel Joy

Your new and fresh approach to joy requires a greater awareness of your feelings.

Be sure to pay more attention to your daily feelings. Pick random moments throughout the day and become conscious of your feelings at the time. Determine how you are feeling— good or not so good. Do your feelings change as the day progresses? If so, what things altered how you were feeling? What things made it harder or easier for you to feel good or not so good?

Secondly, when you find yourself feeling joy, how does that energy feel to you? Does it feel excitable, calm, peaceful or vibrant? Get a sense of the many different sensations that emerge from joy.

The main purpose of this exercise is to help you become more conscious of the fact that your feelings constantly feed your body information.

Opening up your awareness to your daily feelings is an important step in taking self-responsibility for joy.

Keys to the Abundance

- Become mindful of how you feel throughout the day— good or not so good.
- Observe what things affect the way you feel.
- Become aware of the different feelings that you experience, particularly the feelings from which joy arises (e.g. peace, exuberance, vitality, love).

"Fall in love with life by falling into joy. Joy brings lightness to life, it lifts your energy. It has the power to move you away from the heaviness of your mind; it reveals to you the beauty of the world that surrounds you. Joy brings life to your being and your being is the energy of joy. Make it your mission today to be joyful. Place the intention within your mind that today you are going to let go of the emotional heaviness that you carry, instead you are going to listen, feel and live in the energy of joy."

—Words from Spirit

CHAPTER 6

APPRECIATING JOY

"There is so much joy to be felt when you are in vibrational harmony with your being. So much joy."

—Words from Spirit

Our secular world teaches us to rely on our ego as the guiding source by which to live. However there are some pitfalls to living life under the direction of the ego.

The ego works at an emotional level, triggering emotional reactions as a way to respond to life's circumstances. It loves to feel self-important, and it tells us that our opinions are right, that our way of doing things is right. It tells us that in order to experience happiness things need to fall our way. It constantly compares our happiness to the happiness of others. It tells us when life is fair and not fair and when we can be happy and when we cannot.

Our ego keeps us *in search* of happiness *instead of living happily*.

This is its modus operandi and, as a result of its influences, emotionally we are up and down like a yo-yo. One moment our life seems okay; the next moment it's not.

The other problem with the ego is the personal character traits that it fosters. These traits are not helpful or joy-enhancing; they place conditions on our lives and they restrict us from reaching our full potential. Here's a few of them:

- Fear
- Anger
- Greed
- Jealousy
- Envy
- Self-doubt
- Hate
- Resentment

In contrast, the modus operandi of our spirit-self follows a different path. As our spirit-self is of the same essence as the energy of life it's not restricted to a physical body, personality or ego. It's greater than these things.

Being created in the same image as the energy of life the nature of the spirit-self is pure love and joy. As such it guides us to approach life using *character traits that are supportive of joy*, ones that are uplifting and freeing to our life. Here's a few of them:

- Kind-heartedness
- Appreciation
- Love
- Joy
- Self-respect
- Compassion
- Forgiveness
- Truth

These are some of the qualities that our spirit-self houses and employs when called on to help manage everyday experiences.

If you take a moment to re-read the character traits listed for both the ego and spirit-self, you will be able to compare how *differently they feel* within your body. The traits of our spirit-self feel calmer, lighter and positive. They are quite different to the feelings that you experience when you read the traits associated with the ego.

The differences in the feelings that you experience provide you with very important information, namely that unlike the traits of your ego the traits of your spirit-self *feel good.* Their vibes (feelings) *bring harmony* to your whole being—body, mind and spirit—and these vibes bring joy.

Now you may think, *This is all very well, but surely, it'll take a lifetime to master the qualities of the spirit-self.* Well, I have some great news for you. It won't!

By applying to your life one of the jewels within your treasure chest you'll release feelings that'll have you experiencing the vibe of joy (and your spirit-self) in no time at all. This precious jewel is the one known as . . . *appreciation*.

Live Life with Appreciation!

When we live our lives filled with appreciation, not only do we feel better, but we begin to look at life differently.

With new vision we are more inclined to look for the good that occurs each day and relish life's gifts. Our worries don't seem half as bad because our focus shifts to appreciating the good things in our life—the *grace*—and we find joy in the grace!

Appreciation raises feelings and immerses you in joyful vibrations. Learning how to develop 'eyes of appreciation' is one of the easiest, quickest and most effective actions you can take to develop joyful feelings.

Warm-Up Exercise #6: Developing Eyes of Appreciation

Here's a fun practice to help get your appreciation juices flowing. I call this game the *Appreciation Spree Exercise*. It's a top performer. Here's how it works: Each day, spend a couple of minutes listing in your mind all the things that you're appreciative of in your life.

Begin by thinking of the many people you love—family members and friends. Include as many people as you can and hold them with a heart full of appreciation. Then reflect on the grace present in your life. For example, remember the material possessions that you are fortunate to have, the pets that fill your life with love, and the food that you enjoy each day.

Once you have done this, really go crazy appreciating anything and everything that you see in front of you. Yes, everything—flowers, birds, colours, the weather, the sky, the ground beneath your feet, the pen in your hand, the walls of your office, the water you drink, the computer or tablet in front of you, the mobile phone on your desk. Generate appreciative thoughts for anything and everything that you spot with your eyes within a two-minute time frame. Fill two minutes of your life every day with gratitude for absolutely everything.

This practice is one of my favourite joy-enhancing exercises. Often when I do it I have fun by making a game out of it. I set myself a challenge and count how many things I can rattle off during the two-minute cycle. Can I list forty, fifty, sixty expressions or more in gratitude? Wow!

By regularly bombarding your mind in this way you will develop new brain pathways that will steer you towards living life with more gratitude. Also, over time, if you continue with this practice you will assist your brain to release endorphins—the feel-good hormones.

Take the challenge right now. Spend the next few moments listing the things that you're appreciative of in your life. Include family, friends, pets and material items in your expressions of gratitude. Then really let your hair down and have some fun expressing appreciation for everything that you see before you. Don't worry if some of the things you hold gratitude for sound silly. It's not silly to thank the energy of life for everything that exists! In reality what would we do without the ground beneath our feet or the walls and doors in front of us? And what about the chair or bed we are sitting/lying on? Don't these things make our lives more comfortable? Yes, let's give thanks for them too.

Continue the practice daily, expanding, changing and building upon the number of things that you appreciate.

You can raise your spirit and set it free by going on an "appreciation spree!"

Note: Another reason to regularly engage in the act of appreciation is that current neurocardiology research shows that the act of appreciation has positive physiological health benefits to the heart! Fantastic!

Appreciate the Things Present in Your Life Now

Working with the energy of life in better ways is part of our new approach to joy.

Giving thanks for the grace in your life right now is uplifting and it is a key practice that establishes a more positive relationship between you and the energy of life.

For best results this practice needs to be applied in good times and bad—including the times when your wants and desires are not met. Even then, you still need to show your appreciation for *what you have.*

This is essential because the laws of life work in such a way that what we focus on, and give attention to, is created. Therefore, it's important for you to be conscious of the messages that you are sending out to life through your thoughts and feelings. Are you projecting thanks, excitement and appreciation for what you have or feelings of lacking, scarcity and ungratefulness?

Life is an energy responding to the thoughts and feelings of your energy. Therefore it pays to be mindful of the messages that you communicate to life because life is mirroring and responding to the information that you're feeding it.

Give Thanks

It's vitally important to support the feelings of appreciation that you hold with the feeling of *thankfulness*. Both thankfulness and appreciation need to work together in order for the best vibrations to be created.

Take a quick moment right now to say to the energy of life, "I thank you for . . ." (list a personal item that you have). No matter how large or small give thanks for the blessings in your life.

Raising Joy

The quickest thing you can do to feel the joy of your spirit-self in action is to express appreciation and thanks for the gifts in your life.

I cannot overstress the importance of doing this. Appreciation and thankfulness are key players in mastering joy.

"Feel" the joy of appreciation. "Feel" the joy of thanks!

How to Remind Yourself to "Appreciate" the Things in Your Life

Here is a simple way that will help you to remember the daily practice of appreciation. This tip helps to keep the skill alive.

Most of us wear glasses—prescriptive, non-prescriptive or sunglasses. From now on, when you put on your spectacles, use them as a prompt to remind yourself to *look at life through eyes of appreciation.* Use them as a reminder to improve your outlook and vision.

Appreciation is one of joy's jewels. Like a magnet it draws you into the heart of joy. Practised daily it puts you in vibrational harmony with the joy of your spirit-self.

Keys to the Abundance

- Develop the feelings of appreciation through the Appreciation Spree Exercise. This practice brings instant joy and lessens ego-dominated thoughts.
- Appreciation and thanks go hand in hand. Therefore, ensure you hold thoughts of thanks in your expressions of gratitude.
- An item that can prompt you to look at life "through eyes of appreciation" is your glasses/spectacles.

". . . Gratitude lifts you to another vibration. Your
satisfaction and gratitude of all that is in your
life lifts your wellbeing. Instead of focusing on
what you lack, you focus on what you have and
the feelings of gratitude make you become more
aware of the blessings in your life. Gratitude is
healing. It settles the uneasiness within your
being and feeds your cells positive energy.
Be thankful for all that you have."

—Words from Spirit

CHAPTER 7

THE JOY OF PEACE

*"Find a pocket of time each day that allows
you to bring peace and joy to life."*

—Words from Spirit

For many of us life is full and busy, and it's often difficult to find time for peace. However, making time for peace in our lives is an important practice because it helps us experience the diverse feelings of joy.

Before we learn how to incorporate peace into our days, we need to take a look at the requirements and needs of our ego-self—as opposed to our spirit-self—when it comes to sparking joy within us. There is a difference between the two and it pays to be aware of the contrasts.

In order to feel joyful these are some of the things the ego-self needs:

- Things (new car, house, electronics, clothes, ornaments, etc.).
- Experiences (happy ones and ones that go our way, joyful events, achievements, etc.).

- Praise (congratulations, pats on the back, words of encouragement, etc.).
- Perfect relationships (ones that go exactly as we want them to).

In order to feel joyful, this is what the spirit-self needs:

NOTHING! The spirit-self is joy!

As you can see, there is a vast difference between the two. Our ego requires "things" and "experiences" to make us feel joyful. Our spirit-self simply *is* joyful.

Now it is important that I mention here that it is not wrong to have things, happy experiences, great relationships and praise in our lives. Any one of these delights is indeed a great joy-booster! Personal joys bring great happiness to our lives and they're an important part of our life experience.

What is limiting, however, is relying on these personal experiences as sole sources of joy because they restrict our ability to experience joy frequently. They keep us *waiting for joy* rather than experiencing it more often in the present moment.

In order to keep joy palpable throughout our lives we need to know how to access the inner joy of our spirit-self.

How Do We Feel and Recognise the Inner Joy that Stems from our Spirit-Self?

As expressed before, inner joy has many elements to it. It can be felt as energy that is vibrant, exciting and exhilarating. Sometimes the high energy vibration is so full and blissful that you just want to burst out of your skin! It can also be felt as energy that is calming, soothing, peaceful, serene, reassuring and overall positive. Feelings that are simply beautiful.

However, in all of the different ways it expresses itself to us, running through every one of the expressions is a common denominator, namely the feeling of *contentment*.

This is the foremost feeling/energy that inner joy fills your body with. It says to you, "I feel good. This feels so good to me." And this good feeling expresses itself to you as deep contentment.

You know when you are experiencing inner joy when, irrespective of what's taking place in your life, you have an underlying feeling of contentment inside you. Life may be busy. Things may not be as perfect as you want them to be. You may not have everything you want and desire but, nonetheless, you feel good, contented—at peace.

Pausing Is a Necessary Step in the Art of Joy

It's very hard to feel the contentment, the excitement and the gamut of feelings associated with joy if most of the time you are rushing around or if your mind is consistently full of thoughts.

In order to become reacquainted with the feelings of inner joy you need to incorporate 'quiet time' within your daily schedule. Moments of stillness and quietness bring many positive benefits.

Here are some suggestions on how you can grab a few extra moments in your day for stillness so that you can engage in some of the forthcoming peace-filling exercises:

- Watch less television.
- Make it a point to have quiet time before you go to bed, after the children have left for school, or before you start work for the day. It may mean getting up fifteen minutes earlier or spending fifteen minutes less on the computer at night, but the benefits gained will be worth it.
- Make good use of time associated with regular routines. For example, while you are waiting in the car to collect the children from school or while you are catching transport to work, you could use this time to do some of the practices.
- Spend less time each day engaging in social media.
- Schedule time in your diary for *you*. Each day allocate ten minutes of quiet, uninterrupted time. Mark this time off as personal development!
- Make good use of work breaks. Take five to ten minutes of your lunchtime to engage in one of the peaceful exercises that I will soon outline.

Making time for quietness and stillness allows you to become more *au fait* with the language of joy. Yes, there is a *language* to joy. Joy expresses itself and communicates in various ways, not just as happiness but in many other words, thoughts, feelings, patterns, sights and sounds! If we don't take the time to listen to its many expressions, we don't get to experience the full spectrum of joy.

Warm-Up Exercise #7: The Joy of Peace

For this exercise, you will need to find a quiet spot, one that you can return to on a regular basis.

Peace is an expression of the joy of your spirit. To feel this, find a place that you enjoy, somewhere you can sit quietly. Close your eyes. For the next five minutes immerse yourself in one of these techniques:

Technique No. 1: As you sit quietly, breathe slowly and calmly, concentrating on the ebb and flow of your breath. Now breathe in and then release your breath very slowly, allowing the rhythm of your outward breath to take you into a state of peace and deep relaxation. Maintain your focus on your breath, while you calmly inhale and slowly exhale.

Technique No. 2: As you sit quietly, listen to peaceful music. (Ensure the music that you choose is calming to your senses). Whilst you are listening, become aware of the calmness and joy that fills your body. Get lost in the music and its soothing qualities. If you want, you can combine this practice with the first technique, which involves the breath.

Note: Music is a great relaxant that can help stop a busy mind and engender feelings of relaxation. It is possible to incorporate background music into any of the practices that I mention in this chapter.

The goal to work towards is to engage regularly in sitting quietly for five minutes each day. This timely pause will replenish your being and bring balance to your day. You can stop yourself from worrying about running overtime by setting an alarm to ring after five minutes. (Most mobile phones have timers with alarms). Enjoy taking this time for yourself and give thanks for it, as it allows you to "pause" from the merry-go-round of life. What bliss!

Here are some more suggestions on how to grab time for peace each day:

- Walk to a nearby park. Have your lunch break in a park. If you go for a routine jog or walk, stop for five minutes and soak up the beauty of nature. Notice how you feel when you are simply being still and absorbing the glory of creation. Become conscious of the peaceful feelings that arise as you spend time embracing nature.

- Find a pleasant and quiet place where you can sit or lie down. Close your eyes and breathe gently and slowly, and as you do so revisit your treasure chest of joy in your mind. Feel the joyful feelings that come with your image. Make a mental note of any words or feelings that spring forth from your treasure chest as you visualise it.

- If you have a meditation room, a prayer room or a favourite spot in your garden, you can spend the time in your sacred space. How does being in this environment make you feel?

- Meditation is one of the best ways to experience the feelings of inner joy. I have created a short meditative practice that will take less than five minutes of your time each day, and during that time, you will be able to experience inner feelings that elicit joy. You will find this meditation in MP3 format on my website http://www.lightwords.com.au/audio (titled Guided Meditation 5 mins). If you have not meditated before, make sure you listen to the audio titled "Important points to consider before meditating" prior to engaging in the practise. And please don't listen to the meditation while you are driving or operating machinery.

Any one of these exercises will help you. Try them all and find out which ones you really enjoy. Make the ones you like a regular part of your day.

Small pockets of quiet, peace-filled time each day will lift you up and keep you feeling good. Peace brings joy to life.

A Little Warning

Sometimes when we want to make the effort to take 'time out' for peace, we sabotage the moment by making excuses as to why we don't have time for peace.

One way to stop this and get back on track is to reaffirm to yourself that experiencing joy *is* important to you. Then, be firm in your determination and go about your practice. The peaceful feelings that arise from taking some quiet time will be well worth it.

Feel the Joy of Peace

All of the suggested exercises cost nothing, yet they fill you abundantly. They give a depth to your life that no amount of money can buy. It's important to engage in peaceful practices because it's through stillness that we find deeper joy.

There is one more insight that is useful in helping to build our awareness of joy, and it's now time to discover that insight.

Keys to the Abundance

- Make time during the day for moments of peace.
- Five minutes of quiet time each day is all you need to foster peaceful feelings.
- Contentment is the seed of joy. If you work towards attaining the feeling of contentment you'll automatically incite joy.

"Oh Loved Ones, feel the spirit of joy within you. Feel the current of love that runs through your being. All is alive within you. Find the time and the peace to sit still and rest in silence. In the silence feel the wonder of your spirit—joyful, blissful and full of love . . ."

—Words from Spirit

CHAPTER 8

THE HEART OF JOY

*"Be vigilant in monitoring the difference between
what your heart feels and what your mind thinks.*

Your heart feels more than what your mind knows!"

—Words from Spirit

Before we move on to the tools and exercises that will help bring even more joy to our lives, we need to examine one more point—that of where we feel joy.

Heartfelt Joy

Every moment of the day, our feelings are communicating information to us, and the information is *most strongly felt through our heart centre*. The centre of our chest—our heart—is where we "feel" the good feelings and vibrations of joy.

Why Is this Information Helpful?

Knowing *where we feel* joy in our body gives us a reference point. It means that we have a specific location that we can turn to in order to gain feedback on how joyful we are feeling at the time.

How Can this Information Help?

The feelings that we feel around our heart are more closely aligned to our spirit-self. So a way of feeling more from our spirit-self and recognising its presence is to become more *conscious of the feelings that bloom forth from our heart.*

If the feelings that arise from our heart—in conjunction with the thoughts that we are thinking—have loving, joyful, harmonious, peaceful or truthful vibrations about them, we know that the thoughts are more likely to be from our spirit-self than our ego.

Know What's Going on Inside Your Heart

We know our heart is a vital organ that keeps us alive, but there is more to it. Here is what current research is revealing about our heart:

Neurocardiology researchers from the Institute of HeartMath (http://www.heartmath.org/research/science-of-the-heart/introduction.html) have discovered that our emotions and feelings *change the electromagnetic field of our heart.* The atoms of our physical bodies respond to the changes of the electromagnetic field and those changes affect our heart muscle.

When we are stressed, upset, unhappy or not living joy-filled lives the energy field of our heart is affected by the negative emotions that we hold.

The research reveals feelings that improve the energy field of the heart are joy, happiness, appreciation and love.

In other words, all of the *qualities that belong to our spirit-self* feed our heart positive energy and *have beneficial effects on our heart and physical health!*

Wait . . . There's More!

As well as the physical and emotional aspects, researchers at the Institute of HeartMath have compelling evidence that suggests intuitive information is received, processed and decoded by both our heart and brain, but the heart appears to receive the intuitive information first. Our heart "feels" the intuitive information before the thought is received by our brain, and then we gain the insight.

Our heart is an entry point of intuition!

So not only is the heart a muscle that circulates blood around the body, but it is a sensory organ as well. Through its ability to sense emotions it relays information to the brain, which influences the functioning of both the brain and heart. And through its energy field, it has the ability to receive and process intuitive information from our spirit-self.

It's Important to Pay Attention to How You Feel!

As difficult as it may be at times, it is necessary to pay attention to *what* you are feeling and *how* you are feeling. When you are aware of what is going on inside you, you can then take steps towards making improvements to your personal wellbeing, steps that will help you to lessen the emotional baggage that is physically affecting your heart muscle, steps that will make it easier for you to listen to the voice of your spirit-self.

If we look at this information in the context of our personal energy investments (PEIs), we see that our heart is the bank into which our PEIs are physically deposited!

Warm-Up Exercise #8: Heartfelt Joy

This simple exercise is designed to help you become more aware of the physical effects that emotions have on your heart.

Take a quiet moment. Close your eyes and think of a recent situation that left you feeling low in mood. Now place your attention in and around your heart area. Feel what is going on inside your body. Do you feel heaviness in your heart or tightness in your chest? Are the feelings extending beyond the heart region? For example, are they present in the throat area? Do you feel heavy-hearted? Do your shoulders sink? Do you perhaps sigh?

Notice the physical effects of recalling this incident. And in recalling this incident, how close do you feel to the joy of your spirit-self? Do the feelings that you are experiencing feel good—or not so good—to your body, mind and spirit?

Now think of a recent situation that brought you great joy, one that lifted your mood. Once again place your attention in and around your heart area. What is happening to your body this time? Are you feeling warm sensations, lightness of heart? Do you take a breath that causes you to raise your shoulders? How differently does this incident feel to you in comparison to the previous one? Does it make you feel closer to the joy and lightness of your spirit-self? And do the joyful feelings feel good to your body, mind and spirit?

The point of this exercise is to help you realise that your body—especially your heart—*is responding to your tensions and joys*. Your heart tells you if what you are feeling is good for you or not; close to your spirit-self or not. It is a great indicator of our feelings.

In Summary

The more times we feel joy in our heart, the more we improve our health, live through our spirit-self, live with intuition, and work with the attracting forces of energy in positive ways.

The following sections are dedicated to providing you with practical tips and tools that will help you live life with a heart full of joy.

Get ready to improve your life to the max!

Keys to the Abundance

- Become more conscious of the feelings that bloom forth from your heart.
- Become actively aware that every moment of the day your heart is feeling and sensing your emotions.
- Joy improves the energy field of your heart, and it places less physical stress on your heart. Therefore it pays to live life with more joy!

*"As you travel through life do not pack
past frictions and disagreements into your
luggage. Carry only those items that will
help you with your journey each day.*

*Travel light, with preparedness and
with the tools of your heart.*

Peace comes to the well-equipped traveller."

—*Words from Spirit*

PART II

UNDERSTANDING THE THINGS THAT BRING YOU JOY

When you become more aware of the acts of grace that touch your life daily, joy fills your heart.

CHAPTER 9

CREATING YOUR LIST OF JOYS

". . . When you are feeling playful, joyful, know
that these uplifting vibrations are you. Delight
in them and incorporate more of them into
your life and you will move closer to feeling
the joyful nature of the spirit within you."

—Words from Spirit

There are many forms of joy, and in order to learn how to access joy more easily, we are going to begin with a self-awareness exercise that examines the things that bring you joy.

In order to do this exercise effectively, you will be asked to compile a written list. It is important that you write your responses—as opposed to thinking about them. Written answers provide you with information to which you can later refer.

To complete the exercise, you can create a file on your computer or document the information in a journal. Alternatively, visit my website and download the lists titled "Creating Your List of Joys."

The list will be referred to throughout the book, so it is necessary to complete this exercise.

How Long Will This Exercise Take?

Not long. The information that you gain from doing this exercise is valuable as it will help you get to know yourself better. Honour yourself by making time to do the list.

Is the List Worth My Time and Effort?

Yes! Without question! Here are some comments from clients and workshop attendees about the benefits of completing the list:

> *Your list of joys is like a warm blanket—comforting and reassuring! Kaylene*

> *A simple exercise that reminds us of what is important in our lives. How good is that! Sheryl*

By constantly referring to the list of joys it becomes, in time, an automatic response when stressful events present themselves. Irene

Going back to reread a long list of joys is a joy in itself. Janice

It's so easy. You have nothing to lose and so much to gain. Lerae

Your list of joys is a reward to yourself! Margaret

If you want to live a happier life, lower your blood pressure, and have people wonder at what your "secret" is, just do it! Tim

I hope that some positive reinforcement will entice you to undertake this valuable exercise. Let's begin.

Identifying Personal Joys

On the first page, write the words "Personal Joys." You are going to make a list of things in your life that bring you personal joy. This list should include three categories titled:

1. Things I like to do
2. Who I like to be with
3. The material things I have

Write as many items or names as you wish within each of the categories.

Here are some examples from my list that may help to get you started:

1. <u>Things I like to do</u>: Go for morning walks; sit in the sunshine; cook; eat yummy food; spend time with family; take holidays; listen to music; dance; go out for coffee; sing; grow vegetables; take timeout; laugh, laugh, and laugh; watch a good movie; read.
2. <u>Who I like to be with</u>: My husband; our family; our grandchildren; our godchildren; our pet bird, Bella; my school friends; our close friends and my like-minded friends.
3. <u>The material things I have</u> (not what I desire to have but what I actually have): Our home; my car; my clothes; my iPod; the laptop; our oven; our fridge.

You need to ensure the people and items that you list are current. It is important to understand that you are not listing your desires. You are recording worldly experiences that you enjoy, people in your life with whom you enjoy being, and worldly items which you possess that give you pleasure.

This is your personal list, one for your eyes only. The words you write have particular meaning to you. One word may bring you many joys. For example, you may know several things that you enjoy about your car. You could list the aspects individually, or you can simply write the word "car," knowing the many joys it brings.

Ideally, it is best to avoid using long sentences to describe the items or people. Instead, use single words. You can use a bullet-point format or short descriptive statements. Keep it simple.

Also, be honest. Many of us have been indoctrinated into thinking that being spiritual means that we are not allowed to enjoy possessions because in liking them, we become attached to them.

If we are truthful with ourselves, we all have items in our lives that we enjoy, and there is nothing wrong with enjoying them so long as gathering material possessions doesn't become the sole focus and purpose of our lives.

It's okay to appreciate what you have, and indeed, it's necessary to appreciate what you have. Appreciation for the blessings in your life brings joy!

Take your time in creating your list. Once you have done so, read on.

Identifying Inner Joys

Now it's time to go inward and discover inner feelings that fill you with joy. Take a second page and on it write the words "Inner Joys." On this new page you are going to write a list of the things in your life that bring you inner joy. This list should include three categories titled:

1. Inner feelings that bring me joy
2. Things I do to ignite the inner feelings of joy
3. Spontaneous happenings that bring me inner joy

The first category, "Inner feelings that bring me joy," is about discovering feelings that make you feel good *without relying on other people or things.* These are the jewels within your treasure chest, the things that add value to your life.

This section can be a little tricky to complete. To assist you, I'll provide you with some personal examples.

Inner feelings that bring me joy: feelings of peace, love, calmness, contentment, jubilation, playfulness, appreciation, gratitude and equanimity.

I can't buy these feelings. I may not feel them all the time or every day. Yet, when I feel just one of them, it elicits a surge of joy within me. Also the words alone have an energy about them that makes me feel good.

Now it's your turn to document inner feelings that bring you joy. Don't rush. Take your time. When you have completed the exercise, read on.

It is time to develop category two. This is about discovering the things that you do to ignite the "feelings of inner joy" within *you*.

There are certain practices that help you achieve the feelings of inner joy, enjoyable activities that *foster* within you *a peaceful* and *contented state of wellbeing*. You may not have thought about this deeply before. Therefore, to help you think about the activities that stir inner feelings of joy within you, I will provide some personal examples.

<u>Things I do to ignite the inner feelings of joy:</u> meditation, creative visualisation, giving to others, time in nature, surrendering to life, living in the moment, going with the flow, just chilling out, laughing, saying "thank you" more often, making time for myself to watch a sunset or sunrise, pausing to take a moment and give thanks for life, loving myself.

All these things and more help me to feel the delicious inner feelings that I previously listed (calmness, contentment, playfulness, etc.). *They elicit them.* These actions activate the jewels within my treasure chest.

It's time for you to think about the actions that help you achieve the peaceful feelings that you have listed. List what you can and don't get too upset if, for the moment, the list is not comprehensive.

Read on when you have finished.

Okay, we are just about there. The third and final category is about discovering the moments that fall into place *without you having to plan* the precise moment. These *unexpected happenings* fill you with inner joy. They hit the "wow" factor within you. This is when you see the magic of life at work— times when you experience perfect timing or when you just happen to be at the right place at the right moment. You didn't plan it that way. It just happened!

I will start you off with examples that really make me burst with the feeling of joy.

<u>Spontaneous happenings that bring me inner joy:</u> synchronistic and serendipitous moments, coincidences, times when an answer to a problem appears through someone else, moments when I'm out of sorts and suddenly receive an e-mail from a reader that is filled with kindness, times when I think about someone and then receive a phone call from that person.

All these and more press my joy buttons in a huge way. I know that they are *the handiwork* of *the energy of life.*

It's your turn now. See if you resonate with some of the things I have mentioned above. If so, include them as you write your list of unexpected joys.

Fabulous! Before we move on, let's recap.

You should have two pages (or more if you have filled a page during one of the exercises). One marked "Personal Joys," and one marked "Inner Joys."

On the "Personal Joys" page, you have three categories:

1. Things I like to do
2. Who I like to be with
3. The material things I have

On the "Inner Joys" page, you have three categories:

1. Inner feelings that bring me joy
2. Things I do to ignite the inner feelings of joy
3. Spontaneous happenings that bring me inner joy

If you've written only a few examples under each of these headings, do not worry. You are not being tested! The purpose of this exercise is to begin the process of getting to know yourself better and to assist you in finding more joy daily.

From now on, you will become more conscious of recognising what stirs joyful feelings within you—be they from an outer or inner source. When you discover them, add them to your list.

We are going to develop the list a little further. So for now, please keep it with you.

Keys to the Abundance

- Making time to develop your list of joys is an essential step that allows you to access joy more easily.
- There are two main sources from which you can draw that boost your sense of joy:

    o   Personal Joys: These are the things you do, the people you like to be with and the items that you have.
    o   Inner Joys: These are the inner feelings that bring you joy, the activities that ignite these feelings and the synchronistic moments in your life.

- It's helpful to add to your list of joys regularly.

"Joy is found in the simplest of things: a beautiful piece of music; a moment of silence with God; times shared with friends and neighbours. So many times you think your lives lack joy. They don't. If you look for the small pleasures that occur many times during your day, you will see joy delivered in many moments. Be happy. Look for the happiness and joyful experiences that flow through the rhythm of life."

—Words from Spirit

CHAPTER 10

DEVELOPING YOUR
LIST OF INNER JOYS

"To touch another's heart, to bring joy to living,
to love each other and self unconditionally.
These are the reasons for living."

—*Words from Spirit*

When we choose to live with joy and love, oh, how our life improves!

It's time to delve deeper and discover more joy-enhancing qualities that live within us. Now that you have completed the first step towards creating your list of joys, I would like you to spend a moment reviewing both categories. More than likely, you'll have more content listed under "Personal Joys" as opposed to "Inner Joys." That's okay, for this chapter is devoted to helping you further develop your list of *inner joys* and, as such, any entries that you record should be added to your "Inner Joys" list only.

Shortly, you will be presented with some qualities and expressions that evoke inner joy. From the collection that follows, I want you to *add* to your list of inner joys qualities that feel good to you.

You may find that as you read the list you resonate with qualities that aren't present in your life right now. That's okay. Please still include them. This exercise is about discovering the qualities that your heart loves, lives for, and desires. It's about recognising inner knowledge and inner feelings. It's about discovering the jewels of your spirit-self that live within your heart.

How to Know Which Words to Choose

The best way I can describe to you how to choose the words from the forthcoming list is this way: When you read the words and something inside you goes, "Ahhhh," you know those are the words! That particular quality or expression touches you. It sings to your heart and soul, and you sink into the feeling.

Write down as many qualities or phrases under the appropriate categories that *touch your heart*. Avoid thinking about each word or phrase too much. Take each item one at a time and feel them. If one touches you even a little bit, include it within your list and move on.

As you work your way through, feel and trust that your heart is guiding you, telling you, "These things are joyful and meaningful to me."

Category 1: Inner-Feelings

As you read through the list, keep in mind the following statement: "Does this quality feel good to me?" If so, add it to your list. Consider the following words:

- Peace
- Calmness
- Flexibility
- Forgiveness
- Empathy
- Trust
- Playfulness
- Unconditional love
- Nonviolence
- Patience
- Hope
- Happiness
- Serenity
- Appreciation
- Fun
- Strength
- Kindness
- Courage
- Bliss
- Equanimity
- Friendliness
- Spontaneity
- Helpfulness
- Contentment
- Respect
- Integrity
- Caring
- Wisdom
- Warmth
- Harmony
- Kind-heartedness
- Wellness
- Compassion
- Gratitude
- Truth
- Love

- Jubilation
- Grace
- Honesty
- Generosity
- Oneness

More than likely, you would have been drawn to many, if not all of the expressions on the list. This is because every single element is an aspect of your spirit-self. Your heart resonates with these truths. You can feel it because these things feel right, *feel good* to you.

Now that you have developed your list of inner feelings a little further, you have a documented list of values that lead you to feeling joy. You may notice that when you revise your list of inner feelings, you feel contented.

This list touches on some of the qualities that belong to your spirit-self. There are many more. Feel free to include more of them as they come to you.

Category 2: Things I Do that Encourage the Feeling of Inner Joy

As you work your way through the statements listed below, keep in mind the following question: "When I . . . (insert the statement before you) . . . does this activity "bring on" feelings of inner joy?"

- Love
- Feel good about my life
- Accept life
- Surrender to life
- Perform random acts of kindness
- Unclutter my life (emotionally and physically)

- Live truthfully and authentically (with awareness of my spirit)
- Act in playful ways
- Live nonviolently
- Recite affirmations (helpful, positive statements)
- Allow my heart to commune with the energy of life/God/Source/The Universe
- Allow my thoughts to think of the energy of life/God/Source/The Universe
- Live by my personal values
- Feel positive about life
- Fear less
- Worry less
- Live in the moment
- Allow myself to be guided by the energy of life/God/Source/The Universe
- Take time out to feel connected to the energy of life/God/Source/The Universe
- Live peacefully
- Love myself
- Visit a place of worship
- Use tools, such as books or inspirational cards, to keep me inspired
- Remind myself of the abundance that exists in my life
- Make time to just "chill"
- Go on retreat
- Attend inspiring workshops
- Honour myself
- Look for the signs of the energy of life's hand at work
- Co-create positively and deliberately
- Remain open to receiving God's magic
- Play uplifting music
- Spend time in nature
- Make a difference to someone's life
- Believe that help is available to me from the energy of life/God/Source/The Universe

- Trust all timing is perfect
- Live in the now
- Trust life
- Act honestly
- Journal inspiring words that I've read, ones that strike a chord
- Journal my own thoughts and feelings
- Witness life as opposed to getting caught up in it
- Feel good about my actions
- Put the thought "out there" and allow the energy of life to take care of it

If you have resonated with some of the things listed but know that you don't practise or apply them to your life, pay extra attention, for this is your heart pointing out to you that those acts are worthwhile. Your essence is telling you that these are good skills to include in your life.

Once again, I recommend that you add them to your list because they are practices that assist you in feeling inner joy. Including them reminds you that when you engage in these acts, your heart is lifted.

Also, the more practices that you have listed, the more skills you can draw on to help you when the need arises.

Category 3: Spontaneous Happenings that Bring You Inner Joy

This category helps you to recognise the energy effects of joy. By raising your personal energy or vibrations (through joy), you co-create with the energy of life in positive ways. As a result, positive things manifest in your life without you having to orchestrate them!

I call this list the "proof list" because it's proof that your new PEIs are paying off.

Add to your list statements that remind you that when you deliberately live life with more joy, these things are more likely to happen:

- Synchronistic moments
- Positive surprises
- Coincidences
- Help comes to me without me having to organise assistance
- Help comes to me even during the most difficult circumstances
- The right people enter my life
- Impeccable timing (being in the right place at the right time)
- My life improves
- I develop intuition
- Things manifest quickly in my life
- I develop a stronger trust in life
- 'Signs' appear that help and guide me

If you didn't include some of the above within your personal list, please add them because these experiences *will* grace your life when you live from your essence. Adding them to your list will remind you of the positive outcomes that result from changing outdated beliefs and habits.

Now that you have completed this exercise, you should have a well-developed list of inner joys that will give you enough skills to get you started in applying the list to your life. We will learn how to apply the list shortly.

How It All Works Together

When we are guided by inner feelings of joy, personal transformation occurs. You start to worry less, trust life more, live life more with love, feel more peaceful, and feel more *joy*. Perfecto!

And as you play your part and improve your thoughts, feelings and actions, the energy of life responds to the positive changes in your PEIs and, as a result, you see your life improving in positive ways. Here are some examples of how:

Example 1

As you value the inner-joy feeling of *kindness*, you put into action that particular feeling.

For example, you make an effort to perform random acts of kindness on a regular basis. In doing so, the energy of life responds to your thoughts, feelings and actions, and before long you observe unexpected acts of kindness coming back to you!

Example 2

As you value the inner-joy feeling of *peace*, you put into action that particular feeling.

For example, you make the effort to meditate each day. The energy of life then responds to your thoughts, feelings and actions, and you find that not only do you gain peace through meditating, but you gain insights and develop your intuitive abilities as well.

Another example, you make the commitment that you'll try, whenever possible, to maintain your sense of peace, even when people rattle you. As you adopt a more peaceful outlook, you find that people are less angry and irritable towards you.

In summary, the positive changes that you make attract positive experiences to you. More information will come to light as we progress, but for now, it's important to appreciate that when we *value the qualities of joy and do things in our life to support those qualities, life supports us in positive ways!*

The Purpose of the List

Daily pressures often block heartfelt feelings, causing us to forget the many joy-enhancing qualities that are present in our lives.

The list reminds us of what's important in life. It will be used as a tool that will help us worry less, judge others less, and remove belief patterns that take away our enjoyment. It helps us work with the energy of life in positive ways, and most importantly, it enables us to experience joy more often.

It is a powerful list, one we will put to good use.

How to Get the Best out of the List

Over time, expand the personal and inner joy categories on your list. Every now and then, allocate fifteen minutes or more of your time to work on your list. The more detail you have, the more information you have available to help you.

Make sure you keep the list in a place where you can see it or refer to it easily. It is an essential requirement of the "four tools" in the next chapter.

It's time to learn how to apply your list of joys to your life.

Keys to the Abundance

- Every now and then, add to your list of joys. Keep it current and up-to-date.
- Inner joys are the joys that lie at the core of our heart (spirit-self). Therefore, it's particularly helpful to develop this category within the list of joys.
- Keep in mind that when you value the qualities of joy and do things in your life to support those qualities, life will support you in positive ways!

"The joy of the day is felt through the heart. Be in touch with the day. Don't let it pass as just another. Experience it as a precious moment in time that is filled with wondrous moments for you to enjoy.

Fill your day with good intentions. Appreciate it, and you will delight in life."

—*Words from Spirit*

PART III

THE FOUR TOOLS AND FOUR FACTORS THAT LEAD TO A JOY-FILLED LIFE

Make it your mission to be joyful. Place the intention that today you are going to let go of emotional baggage. Today you are going to feel and live in the energy of joy.

CHAPTER 11

THE FOUR TOOLS

*"In the 'now,' think of something that brings
you joy; and then become conscious of how
you feel when you reflect on the joy.*

*This technique of now joy, feel joy, or, if it is easier
for you to remember—now feel the joy—will lift
you from your negative feelings and bring you
back to creating positive changes in your life."*

—Words from Spirit

In receiving writings from *Spirit* for many years now, I have come to appreciate that whenever they provide exercises, tips or tools to help us with our life journey, they are usually uncomplicated and simple to follow. If we take the above message as a case in point and summarise what *Spirit* are saying to us, we conclude that the best thing we can do in any moment is to *now feel the joy!*

So, to enable you to do just that, I am going to introduce you to four special tools.

These tools are easy to apply and they complement the work that you have done so far in the previous two chapters. I will explain each one in detail. It is helpful to note that the explanations may appear lengthy, but the application of the tools is quick and easy. The truth is, using the tools is much easier than writing about them!

Tool 1

This tool is about observing your thoughts.

The purpose of this tool is to help you become more aware of your daily thoughts, witness your thoughts and their effect on your wellbeing, and gain awareness into the way that your mind responds to the changing circumstances of your life.

How does the tool work? Through the act of witnessing your thoughts you gain valuable information. You learn to recognise if the thoughts that you hold are helpful or detrimental to your sense of wellbeing. Are they inhibiting your ability to feel joy? Are they preventing you from manifesting positive things in your life? Are they repetitive, habitual, fearful or worrisome?

It's important I stress that the aim of this tool is to observe your thoughts, *not judge them*. You are not analysing "how" or "why" you are thinking those particular things. Your goal is to simply *be aware* of what you are currently thinking.

It's not until we're aware of our thought patterns that we can take the steps to alter them. More often than not *it's our thoughts*, not our current circumstances, that deprive us of the experience of joy.

Therefore the first tool, which develops mindful awareness, is essential in helping us take steps towards positive change.

Tool 2

This tool is about measuring your feelings.

The purpose of this tool is to provide an evaluation system that allows you to measure your feelings.

How does this tool work? The visual aid prompts you to instantly identify how you are feeling. Are you close to joy or distant from it?

The process is simple. You tune into your feelings and grade them on a scale of one to ten. The more joyful and vibrant you feel, the higher the reading; the less joyful, the lower the reading. You make a mental note of the measurement.

Becoming aware of our feelings provides us with more information about why we are experiencing less joy in our lives. How we feel is paramount to our experience of joy. When we are out of sorts our focus is often on the chatter in our head, but we need to know what's going on in our *heart* too! Allocating a numeric value to the feelings you hold gives you a reference point from which you can improve your situation.

Ideally this tool works best if you keep an image of the scale in prominent places. Personally I keep one in my office, car and purse. When I see the image I am reminded to "check in" and see how much joy I am feeling in the moment. This allows me to make changes if my reading comes up short.

To begin with I recommend that you record at least one reading each day for a month. This will help you become more conscious of what feelings you hold. Keep your notations short, sharp and simple, and make a note of what affected your feelings at the time. Was it a thought? Was it your reaction to a situation that made you feel worse or better?

Also make sure you record the positive changes that you instigated in response to your readings. It's great to look back on the times that prove to you that you are taking steps towards positive change.

A daily record will give you insight into your emotional body, allowing you to improve your inner feelings if need be. For ease of documentation, visit my website for a downloadable spreadsheet titled "Charting My Daily Feelings."

Tool 3

NOW

This tool is about present awareness.

The purpose of this tool is to bring your attention to the fact that you can change how you think and feel right now. This tool reminds you that "now" is the most powerful moment in your life to embark upon change.

How does this tool work? After you have observed your thoughts and measured your feelings, the image of the word "now" will remind you it's time for action! It prompts you to ask, "What can I do right now to raise my thoughts and feelings?"

It also raises the question of *how—right now*—can you improve the way you think and feel?

Tool 4

This tool is about taking positive action that works well for you.

The purpose of this tool is to give you a framework to draw on in order to bring joy back to your life.

How does this tool work? Each item on your list of joys is meaningful to you. As such, it reminds you that you can ignite joy by simply applying different elements from your list to your life.

As you turn to the list for help, you will be drawn to different aspects from both sides—personal and inner joys. Changing circumstances in your life will mean that you apply the list in different ways. At times you may start with things listed under the heading of personal joys. Sometimes the opposite will occur, and many times you will draw from all areas of your list of joys.

How you work the list is not prescriptive. But, like any tool, you need to use it in order for the tool to be effective.

How to Action Your List within the Four Tools

Here is an illustration of how you can implement the four tools. Let's say an unexpected event alters the plans that you had for the day. As a result, your day is turned upside down.

<u>Tool 1</u>: Observe your thoughts. More than likely you'll feel yourself expressing annoyance, disappointment and frustration. (The ego is quick to express its disapproval when things don't go to plan).

<u>Tool 2</u>: You measure your feelings and register them as a number. For the sake of this exercise we'll say that your reading is down to 3.5 on the scale.

<u>Tool 3</u>: This tool reminds you that you can change your thoughts and feelings about this situation right now. It reminds you that it's now time for action!

<u>Tool 4</u>: In your mind you reflect on your "list of joys." You know that you can start in any of the categories on the list, but if you start with inner feelings that bring you joy, you'll determine a goal to work towards. So you know that you want joy and you choose feelings that will take you to joy (e.g., peace and calmness).

Once you have decided on the feelings you look at ways to create the peaceful inner feelings. This may include activities like one-minute breathing exercises to bring calmness to your body or affirmations (positive statements) to bring more peaceful thinking.

There are things you like to do that can help you right now. For example, listening to music can shift a mood and so can being in nature. Sure you may not have the time to go and sit in a park for twenty minutes, but stepping outside for just a moment and filling your lungs with a breath of fresh air could just be the fix you need to release tension and improve the way you feel.

As you do so you could reflect on synchronistic events and be reminded that, even though the day has turned out differently than you expected, you have the power to help improve the situation. You can do this by projecting thoughts to the energy of life that from now on your day improves. You can support these thoughts by mentally visualising the rest of the day unfolding smoothly.

You think about the people you love to be with in your life, and as you attend to your change of plans, these people come to mind. Just thinking about them gives you good feelings. Alternatively you could think of someone you regard as a role model—a spiritual teacher, for example—and reflect on how this person would respond to and manage the situation that you face.

Life continues. The day is busy. What items do you have that could help you manage the day more easily? Your car, for example, takes you where you need to be faster than public transport. Wow, how lucky you are to have that car! A computer program helps you work more efficiently than the need to finish the current task by hand.

The feelings of appreciation for the things that grace your life raise your spirits. When you realise this you check in and see that your feelings are a little calmer than when you first began.

Your list reminds you that, at any time, you can ask for help from the energy of life with regards to the situation that you are facing. You could, for example, ask (and visualise) that you get green traffic lights as you drive to your destination so that your journey is a quick and easy one. Or maybe you need assistance from others (a babysitter for example), and as you make phone calls to find the help you need, you can put the thought "out there," asking life to assist you with the matter at hand. Your mind starts thinking about possibilities, help and synchronicity.

You realise that taking positive action in whatever form that works for you raises your feelings and levels of happiness.

As the day unfolds and you go about your activities you check within and revisit tools 1 and 2. You observe that your mind is still busy, but less so. You note that your feelings have lifted and now you give them a value of 7.0. This means you have progressed forward—this is good! Again, you draw upon things that you enjoy in order to help improve your mood.

And as you continue to apply different aspects of your list of joys to your life you begin to feel better, calmer, and, overall, more peaceful and joyful than you were when you first began. The end result of doing this is that you are less reactive and more proactive. Your mind is less focused on the bleats of the ego and more focused on thoughts that direct you towards making the best of what's happening in your life right now.

So, in this illustration, you were able to draw upon strategies and values in all categories of your list of joys, strategies that helped you to feel better. You used the *inner feelings of peace and calmness* to lift you back to joy. You reminded yourself of the *things you have* that help you live an easier life. (Cars and computer programs were the two examples given). You used personal skills to help you *ignite the feelings of inner joy*—breathing techniques, visualisations and affirmations. You drew on things that you love *to do* to help lift your mood. (Music and nature were the examples used). You called on the energy of life to help you, and you looked for the *signs* of confirmation (e.g., the green traffic lights, the help that came to hand, the day unfolding smoothly). You thought about the people in your life who fill you with happiness. Just the thought of them helped you.

Throughout the day you sourced and applied different strategies from your list of joys to help you create a more positive day.

In this particular example it is worth noting that you did not have to take extra time out of your day to apply the strategies. "I'm too busy to think about these things right now" is a common *excuse* that stops us from applying new strategies to our life.

As you can see in this illustration, I have shown you how it's possible to incorporate elements of your list of joys into whatever you are doing. Yes, it is possible to apply many of the practices without drawing on extra time!

Personal Change Takes Time!

Let me reassure you again. It is easier to apply the four tools than it is to read about them. The first step is to simply give them a go.

In regards to the fourth tool, your list of joys, focusing on the category "inner feeling that brings you joy" is often a great place to start. Sometimes though, if our emotions are high, starting with this section can be difficult. If this is the case then turn to a category that is manageable for you. Choose something that you can sink your teeth into straight away. If that activity starts the process of changing your behaviour, then that is good.

Like all new things, mastering the list will take a little practise. To begin with, it's a good idea to have your list of joys in an accessible place so that you can refer to it frequently. Over time you'll easily recall the different elements that you have listed but, initially, keep the list handy.

Changing old habits does take time and effort. However the *four tools help lessen the time it takes to change old habits*. They do this by guiding you through a formula that leads to practical outcomes.

I know how much the four tools have helped me with my life. As an author, my time to write often gets taken away by the other roles that I play in life—business owner, employee, wife, daughter, stepmother, step-grandmother, nurse, volunteer. In days of old, when I had a day planned for writing and things went pear-shaped, I would have reacted to the change of plan. The "old me" would have harboured a bad mood. Feelings of anger and resentment would have stayed with me all day. My mind would have repeated a thousand times, "You'll never get this book finished."

However, the four tools have changed my reactions and habits. They have taught me to take responsibility for the way that I think and feel. They have engendered within me a healthier mental, emotional, physical and spiritual state through the power of joy.

Now, as I use the four tools, I let my initial reaction from my ego surface. I witness it and then get on with improving how I feel. This becomes my priority—not my ego but *my desire to feel joy*.

"Now feel the joy" becomes the goal that I work towards. For joy is important to me; it's my daily destination!

In Summary

These tools provide you with an effective, transformative, step-by-step process.

Tool 1 examines your current thoughts. It gets you to *see* what's going on in your mind (not judge, just witness).

Tool 2 measures your feelings. *Your feelings* determine your level of joy.

Tool 3 is the point of change. It reminds you that it's up to you to improve your thoughts and feelings.

Tool 4 is *your action plan*. Through your list of joys you are able to identify and engage in personal strategies that can improve how you feel.

Your goal is to work both sides of your list of joys so it helps you shift away from reactive emotions of the ego into the joyful energy of your spirit-self.

The Application

Examine your thoughts

Measure your feelings

Now

Use your list

As you become proficient in using the four tools, you will find that just one image of the tools will systematically move you through them. Well-practised, the four tools will become second nature to you. They are a lifeline to joyful living!

The four tools can best be summarised in one easy statement: *Check your thoughts and measure your feelings; now use your list to guide you!*

How good is that!

Keys to the Abundance

- The four tools are designed to raise self-awareness.
- When you want to lift your mood and feel more joyful apply the four tools.
- Keep a list of the four tools handy. This will help remind you to use them during the day.

"There are many moments on the path that bring joy—none more powerful than when you observe positive changes in your behaviour. Changes that say to you, you are making steps towards spiritual consciousness.

Celebrate the joy of your spiritual growth and development. Feel the positive energy you fill yourself with as you celebrate. Carry this joy and you will want more and more each day to move forward along the path.

Raising your awareness is exhilarating."

—*Words from Spirit*

CHAPTER 12

USING TOOL FOUR EFFECTIVELY

"You will be amazed at the events that occur in your favour when you let go of the reins and allow."

—Words from Spirit

Tool four, your list of joys, is a great tool that helps you work with the energy of life in positive ways. It is designed for you to get the best out of the physical experience so that your energy works in sync with life. Living this way is a lot more fun than being in "control mode" all the time!

The Overall Purpose of the List

Your list is a reminder to you of the things in life that you value.

Each category within the list has a specific purpose.

What Is the Purpose of the List of Personal Joys?

So many times we feel that if we had more in our lives we would be happier. Our longings often take us away from the enjoyment, satisfaction and appreciation of what we already have.

In different ways and to different degrees, all of us have things in life that we value. Good health, our home, our loved ones, the education that we've had, our career, our personal skills, the special friendships we have, our pets. Any of these things can be seen as grace in our life.

The list of personal joys engenders appreciation. It reminds us of the riches that fill our life and of the presents that fill our present!

How to Approach the Three Categories within the List of Personal Joys

Things I like to do: The purpose of this section is to remind you of all the activities that you like doing and are capable of doing.

When you want a quick lift, come to this part of the list. Select and engage in one of your favourite activities. This will give you a boost.

As you review this section you may discover that some forgotten activities suddenly spring to mind. If this is the case, add them to your list. In doing so, you will be reminded to include them in your life again. They are special joy-boosting practices that you know bring joy to your life.

This section opens your eyes to the many different activities available to you that make you feel good. When you feel good, you have the strength to manage the circumstances of your life in more productive ways.

<u>Who I like to be with</u>: We all have people in our lives who lift our spirits and whose company we enjoy. Partners, family members, and like-minded friends are all essential to our physical and spiritual wellbeing.

Use this area of the list to remind yourself of the many people who grace and inspire your life. Reflecting on the people close to your heart reminds you of the great joy held in friendships.

We all have role models and inspiring teachers in our lives. Ensure you include them in this category too, for recalling them can often encourage you to deal with life circumstances in loving and inspiring ways.

And remember to include your favourite pets in this section. There is nothing more precious than spending time with loving pets. Their unconditional love lifts our heart and fills our joy tank immeasurably.

This section helps you become aware of the preciousness of good friendships and the love that surrounds your life.

<u>The material things I have that I enjoy</u>: When something has robbed you of feeling joyful, come to this list and reflect on your material possessions, especially the ones that make life easier for you. See if you can use one of them to give yourself a lift. As an example, I enjoy cooking, and sometimes when I need to ignite feelings of joy I will cook something (usually a cake) in our oven. I get so much pleasure from our oven. Having had a couple of not so good ones over the years, this one is a sheer delight. There isn't a time when I use it that

I don't thank the energy of life for the gift of having that appliance in our house.

When we appreciate the things that we have, including everyday household items, we get so much more enjoyment from using them.

This section helps you see the many material blessings in your life. It promotes and develops the powerful qualities of gratitude and appreciation.

What Is the Purpose of the List of Inner Joys?

This is the heart of your list, your treasure chest! This is where you really get to feel joy at its best. These are the feelings that touch you deeply. They are the things that move you closer to feeling your spirit-self.

How to Approach the Three Categories on the List of Inner Joys

The inner feelings of joy: This section reminds you of the values and feelings that lift your heart. This is where *joy really is* for *you*. All of the other categories are working towards helping you achieve the feelings that you have listed in this section.

It is advisable to read this category frequently. This will ensure that, whatever activity you undertake, it will touch and stir some of the feelings on this list. This is important.

As previously mentioned, it is helpful to make this section your starting point. Begin by asking yourself, "What do I want?" Answer, "Joy!" and then go through your list of inner feelings and determine which ones you are drawn to. Those inner feelings are the ones you work towards, and you use elements from *all* of the other categories to help you feel those inner feelings.

You will find that, depending on the circumstances, some inner feelings are more appropriate to work towards than others. Each time, choose the inner feelings that you believe to be the most beneficial to you at the time.

Things I do to ignite the inner feelings of joy: This section is where you come to support all those delicious inner feelings that you love to feel. These practices are the ones that ignite them, that really do it for you.

Ideally, these are the activities and practices that you turn to most. That is not to say the others don't have their places. They certainly do, but *these* practices are the crème de la crème when it comes to igniting inner joy!

Spontaneous happenings that bring me inner joy: This section is the one you come to for motivation. It spurs you to embrace joy because you know that when you do, amazing things will happen in your life.

Motivate yourself as often as possible by reviewing this category each time you read your list.

As an extra incentive, when amazing things do happen in your life, such as coincidences or moments of perfect timing, add the event to your list. Proof and confirmation that you are in sync with the energy of life is exciting. The bonus of doing this is that when you re-read your own personal experiences, you relive them. This not only creates inner excitement and joy, but it helps you create thoughts and feelings that draw more of these episodes to your life.

There is nothing more exhilarating than when we see the energy of life's hand at work. Experiencing these times and reflecting on them is a real buzz!

A Guide to Using Tool Four

Here is a step-by-step guide that will help you optimise your list. Firstly, always keep in mind that when you are using the list, you are trying to achieve this statement: "Now feel the joy." With this goal in mind, consider the following steps:

1. Go to your list.
2. Look at what you have written under personal joys and inner joys.
3. *Feel* what actions/practices are right for you *at the time.* (They will differ with each experience).
4. Ask yourself what activities/practices are going to promote warm feelings of inner joy.
5. Ask yourself what is possible and practical for you to engage in right now.
6. Ask yourself if there are some things that you can do later in the day in order to continue to raise your feelings towards joy.
7. Decide if it's beneficial for you to participate in more than one activity right now. If so, how can you make it happen?
8. Check within to see if you are in the right frame of mind to participate in the activity that you have chosen. For example, trying to meditate when your mind is going stir crazy is not easy. You may gain more benefit from participating in another activity that will lift you and then meditating when you are more settled. The aim is to achieve what you want to achieve in practical ways.

9. Re-read the third category on your list of inner joys as often as possible. Confirmation that you and the energy of life are working together is uplifting and fun.

Some Practicalities

- Before using tool four, your list of joys, it's always a good idea to firstly run through tools one, two and three.

  - o   Tool 1: Examine your thoughts
  - o   Tool 2: Measure your feelings
  - o   Tool 3: Now
  - o   **Tool 4: Use your list**

- Refer to your list of joys regularly.
- Add to it as often as you can. The more comprehensive the list is, the better it is for you. This will provide you with a wide range of options that you can apply to the variety of situations that you encounter.
- Don't try to do too many things at once. This may cause you to become stressed. The idea is to ignite joy, not stress!
- Tailor your responses to the different challenges you meet.
- Enjoy participating in the activities/practices. See them as the best part of your life. View this list as your lifeline.
- The first step is to engage in an activity that lifts you closer to feeling joy. Then keep momentum flowing and work through practices that continue to ignite inner joy.
- Always keep in mind that the action you take needs to be sustainable, enjoyable and achievable.
- Have fun with this tool. Use it in creative ways.
- And most of all . . . keep it handy!

It Helps to Put It "Out There."

When there is a problem in my life, I often engage in the practice of asking the energy of life to solve the problem for me. I put the thought *out there* that help will come to me or that my problem will be solved. I stay positive by *trusting* that the energy of life *will* help me. I release my request with love and, once that's done, I engage in things from my list of joys that keep me in a joyful state.

So often, when I let go and trade my worries for joy, the most miraculous occurrences take place. More often than not, the perfect solution to my problem appears—one that I hadn't planned or thought about.

Putting your requests 'out there,' trusting that a solution will arise; releasing your problems while deliberately staying in the energy of joy is a great practice that supports your list of joys. It creates magical moments.

And when you work with life in this way, remember to thank the energy of life for the help given. Gratitude is vital, and the more excited you feel when you give thanks, the better!

Enjoy working with the four tools, particularly your list of joys. Enjoy how they raise you up back into the energy of joy.

I suggest that before reading further you take the time to assimilate the four tools.

Once you are clear about them, join me in discovering the four key ingredients that power the four tools.

Keys to the Abundance

- The joys listed under the heading of personal joys engender appreciation. Therefore, turn to these categories to remind yourself of the many riches that fill your life.
- The joys listed under the heading of inner joys engender higher feelings. Therefore, turn to these categories to raise and uplift yourself in joy.
- For optimum effect, use tool four in conjunction with tools one, two and three.

"Do not sleep through life. Awaken yourself to the spirit within. Allow that part of you to come alive. Understand who you really are and make your decisions and choices through the higher part of you.

You are greater than you realise yourself to be."

—Words from Spirit

CHAPTER 13

THE FOUR FACTORS

"There is only one way to march through
life and that is forward with love.

Let love be yours."

—*Words from Spirit*

Love is the most powerful force there is. If we want to get the best out of life and increase our sense of joy, then there is one essential step that we need to take, and that is to increase our ability to love.

Let's look at how we can do that.

At this point, we have four tools that can help us to experience more joy. The four tools are practical, useful and easy to apply. Can we live by them alone?

The four tools take giant steps towards raising our level of joy. However, if you really want to maximise their effect, more is required. I'll show you why.

Let's say that someone has acted nastily towards you. The person's words and actions have left you feeling hurt and offended. Armed with just the four tools, you could respond to this incident in the following manner.

You observe your thoughts and note that they replay the scenario over and over again in your mind. You measure your feelings. Your feelings of hurt and anger result in a low reading. So you take action—now. You go to your list of joys, and from it, you choose a response that will help to calm and bring better feelings to your heart. For the sake of this exercise we'll say that you decide to go and sit in a park.

You do so, however, after a while in the park you discover that your mind is still going crazy. You are so pent up that, even though you have taken action by going to the park—which is something that usually makes you feel good—little has changed. You have removed yourself from the scene, but the pain and anger have travelled with you!

So with this example you have followed the four tools, but it appears that you have not benefited from using them. And my guess is that even if you engaged in other activities from your list of joys to help you, those activities will only lift you temporarily. Why?

Your emotional response to the incident is predominantly under the guiding influence of your ego. It's calling the shots. Unless you draw from a source of power other than ego, the four tools will not be effective in the *long term*.

The good news is there is help at hand.

There are four factors that both improve the performance of the four tools and lessen ego consciousness. These higher understandings, which stem from the heart of our spirit-self, determine the *success* of the four tools. Let's become acquainted with them.

Relationship

This first factor is about honouring and nourishing the relationship that you have with the energy of life. As previously mentioned you may call and understand the energy of life as Source, God, Divine Love, The Universe, Consciousness, etc. It doesn't matter what you call or perceive the energy of life to be. What does matter is that you acknowledge it in your life! That you develop an awareness of the interconnected relationship that you have, and you build your relationship on a *foundation of love and friendship*, as opposed to fear and separation.

The boons of integrating this relationship into your life are many. It adds a deeper dimension to living. It makes you consciously aware that you are not alone. Help, from a higher source, *is* available. When you walk hand in hand each day in recognition that you and the energy of life are in partnership together, your life has meaning and focus.

In building this relationship, qualities such as love, peace, contentment, trust, acceptance, friendship, strength and courage emerge. These are powerful qualities that can help support you throughout life.

How does this awareness help power the four tools? When we plug into relationship we are reminded that we are not alone in life, not alone in our problems and worries. *Help* is available to us. And we can draw on the help any time because that help is just a thought or a feeling away.

Oneness

The second factor involves seeing the link that we have to each other. We may see ourselves as independent beings, but we are connected. One chord of life, one energy connects and sustains us all.

As such, what we do and say affects others.

I like to picture it this way. It is not possible to pull a single strand of spaghetti out from a bowl of spaghetti without that strand touching and affecting other strands. That's our lives in a nutshell. Everything we do, think and feel touches others in life.

This insight develops qualities within us like respect, acceptance, compassion, tolerance and understanding towards others. It reduces the need to lay blame. Through oneness we see a bigger picture to life.

How does this awareness help power the four tools? When we plug into oneness, we expand our thinking and see that our personal actions, moods and life responses affect not only ourselves but others too! When we are conscious of *the bigger picture*, we are more likely to take the initiative to improve the way we think, behave and act. Another key element to oneness is that it stops us from acting in selfish and self-centred ways.

Love

Out of all the factors, the third factor is the one with the highest voltage! Love changes lives, and we best experience our full potential when we feel, think and act through love—unconditional love.

When love is the motive behind our thoughts, feelings and actions, we view life more positively and live it that way too.

This insight develops qualities like joy, compassion, tolerance, forgiveness, harmony, peace, self-acceptance, non-violence, gratitude, appreciation, happiness, integrity, honesty, and the list goes on! Any of these qualities can transform our life.

How does this awareness help power the four tools? Love is the greatest power of all, and when we plug into it, it *heals and transforms* our personal responses. Embracing this factor alone results in great personal transformation.

Energy

The fourth and final factor is the *core awareness* that all other factors are built upon. It's the understanding of energy. Everything in life is created from energy. We communicate with the life force through energy.

Appreciating this fact allows us to be more discerning of the messages we communicate daily through the energy of our thoughts, feelings and actions. Our aim is to improve them and to become more conscious of and deliberate about what we choose to think, feel and do.

The first three factors help us achieve this goal. They direct us towards making the best use of energy.

This insight develops qualities that are positive, and we know that we want to live by positive qualities because they are the values that lead us to joy.

How does this awareness help power the four tools? We are more inclined to put our personal energy to good use. We have a desire to create positive outcomes in our life because we know that by doing this, we are more likely to *attract* positive outcomes.

The four factors are key understandings that help get the best out of the four tools. They are the *awareness you draw on* as you live your life and as you apply the tools.

How to Remember the Four Factors

Now this may seem like an awful lot of information to remember, but I'm going to make it very easy for you. By taking the first letter from each word of the four factors, we create the acronym ROLE:

Relationship
Oneness
Love
Energy

Therefore, to remember each of the four factors, simply think, "ROLE!"

Recalling ROLE as you apply the four tools will raise your thinking. These higher thoughts lead to better management. At times, the ego will interject the higher thoughts, but if you keep reflecting on the four factors and draw on them, your perspective will change. You will find that you respond more effectively—less from the ego and more from your spirit-self.

Shortly, I will give you some suggestions that will help you apply ROLE in practical ways, but for now, let's go back to our scenario at the beginning of this chapter and see what happens when we add the four factors to the equation. Let's see how they raise our thinking.

In the park, as your mind replays the scene and the feelings of hurt surge, you call to mind the four factors. In doing so, your focus starts to shift a little.

Initially, thoughts arise that question, "How can I deal with this differently, more effectively?" "What can I do to stop my mind from going over this a thousand times?"

Then, as you break the word ROLE down letter by letter, you may find yourself reflecting on your relationship with the energy of life. You'll remember that this energy is available to help, support and guide you through this situation. You'll think about your actions and responses, how they affect you, and how they affect other people in your life. These thoughts prompt you to respond to the situation in a responsible way. You'll remember that love can help you, and you'll look at options that will walk you down the path of love. You will have the awareness that you want to work positively with the energy of life, and you will think about ways to achieve this through higher thoughts, better feelings and enlightened actions. You'll think about your personal energy investments and how you can improve them through love and joy.

The questions and thoughts that arise will be different for each of you, but the outcome will be the same. ROLE will lift your thinking. It does this by stopping the repetitious nature of the mind and giving it a higher focus to think about. This change of direction helps to shift you away from the bleats of the ego.

The four factors *talk differently* than ego. They say to you, "Hey, what can I do to move through this situation or improve it so I can get back to feeling joy again?" They tell you to draw on greater resources than that of ego's emotions, and they tell you what those resources are; namely relationship, oneness, love and energy.

They ensure that instead of letting things get the best of you, *you give them your best!*

Once you engage in the four factors, all sorts of questions will sprout forth. Each time you revisit the scenario from a higher perspective, you are presented with the possibility of taking action that results in you holding less anger, hurt, fear and frustration.

The four factors promote self-responsibility, positive conflict resolution and less emotional injury. They guide and drive you to engage in healthier attitudes and outcomes.

More Reasons Why the Four Factors Are Important

The four factors set the motives and intentions behind our actions. They ensure that we don't develop selfishness and self-centred attitudes. Some people could interpret "taking personal responsibility for joy" with an attitude that says, "*It's all about me*. My sense of joy is all that matters. I don't care about others; I'm just going to do the things that please me."

The four factors stop selfish attitudes such as these from developing. They encourage us to look at the bigger picture, and see how life fits together. Improving our lives through joy is not about abdicating our responsibilities and living life indulging our desires and senses. It's about facing up to our responsibilities, managing life through the good and challenging times, *taking the initiative* to apply life skills that support sound personal energy investments, ones that are positive and helpful to ourselves and others.

The four factors promote these things and more.

Lessening Ego Control

As you place your focus of attention on the four factors, ego-driven habits will fall away. It takes practice to think in this new way. However, the more you recall ROLE, the more you create new pathways in your brain that lead to improved habits.

ROLE quickly brings to mind things that are of value to our spirit-self. Its simplicity cuts to the chase, bringing together key life principles, spiritual practices and universal laws in a way that can be easily remembered and applied.

The four factors support the four tools by ensuring that we operate from the higher mind of our spirit-self.

The Change in Thinking

The four factors foster positive belief systems. Through them we value:

- Love
- Joy
- Truth
- Peace
- Unity
- Non-violence
- Oneness
- Right action
- Awareness
- Acceptance
- Compassion
- Forgiveness
- Our relationship with life
- Self-respect (including respect of our spirit-self)
- Self-care (loving towards ourselves)
- Self-responsibility (being responsible for our own thoughts and actions)

All of these things hold positive vibrations that lift our consciousness. They bring balance and harmony to our lives returning us to *joy*.

Through them, we move away from:

- Hate
- Envy
- Anger
- Blame
- Judgements
- Dominance
- Fear
- Jealousy
- Greed
- Resentment
- Hurt
- Criticism
- Selfishness
- Comparison with others all the time
- Resistance to change
- Abuse of the earth
- Self-abuse (ignoring our spirit-self)

All of these things hold negative vibrations that keep us in ego-consciousness. They have us working in opposition to the flow of life. They bring *pain*.

In Summary

The four tools are the *action* that you take. The four factors are the *awareness you draw on* as you put the tools into action. The following chapter is dedicated to practical tips that will help you incorporate and apply the principles of ROLE.

Keys to the Abundance

- The four factors (ROLE) are key life ingredients.
- For maximum effect, apply the four factors to the four tools.
- The four factors are *the awareness* you hold that result in a change of perspective. When you change your perspective, you change everything!

"Differences between people; there are many differences between individuals but the differences stem from the personality.

In truth all are the same; all are from the one Source and cosmic energy. All are created equally from the energy of love. The ego and personal identity are the forces that separate you from who you truly are.

Lessen the ego; unite with Source and you are well on the road to reclaiming your being."

—Words from Spirit

CHAPTER 14

APPLYING THE FOUR FACTORS

*"Without joy, there is no love. Joy
brings love and love brings joy."*

—*Words from Spirit*

A key point to the four factors is that their power lies in your *awareness* of them. They are mindful thoughts that you hold onto, thoughts that you are *aware of,* as you engage in your daily activities.

This is a crucial understanding. Your awareness of the four factors holds power because they cause you to think, feel and act from a higher perspective—in harmony with your spirit-self. The more conscious you are of the four factors, the more you'll naturally apply them to your life.

So, how can you become more conscious of the four factors so that you are more likely to apply them? Here are some creative suggestions:

Suggestion 1—Use an Action Statement

Actions statements are helpful to reinforce certain points in our minds. Here is a statement that will remind you of ROLE and describe to you how to play your role in life.

Affirm: "My role (in life) is to recognise that I am in a *relationship* with the *one loving energy*."

Recalling this statement raises awareness, and it reminds us that one of the purposes of our lives is to use our personal energy in loving ways.

To really enhance the statement, begin by asking yourself this question: "What is my role?" Then reply, "My role is to recognise that I am in a *relationship* with the *one loving energy*."

Then, as you put into action the four tools, keep the four factors in mind, allowing them to guide your responses and actions.

Reminding ourselves that our role in life is to respond to life in higher ways is an effective technique that can lead to improved actions and outcomes and lessen ego-consciousness.

Suggestion 2—The Right Power Source

When you think about tools in general, you are reminded that all tools need a power source. Power is what brings a tool to life and it's what makes a tool work so that you are able to use it to the best of its ability.

The same fact applies to the four tools. The power source they need to operate well is *ROLE power!*

Viewing *ROLE power* as the power source for the four tools makes it easier to grasp how the four factors support the four tools. Quite simply they are the power source that brings the tools to life!

Suggestion 3—Picture the Big Moment

We have all seen images where an illuminating thought, a brainwave of an idea, is depicted by a light-bulb moment.

Each time you use the four tools, recall the image of the light bulb. Let the image remind you that clarity, illumination and enlightened thinking all stem from ROLE. Then apply the principles of ROLE to your actions.

Extra tip: This image is a useful one to recall any time that you need help in your life. When you need guidance, think of the light-bulb image, call ROLE to mind, and allow the four factors to help you through the situation that you are facing.

New Habits

All of these suggestions are designed to create new habits that help train your mind to respond in higher ways. They help ensure that the new tools you are applying to your life are powered and supported by new practices.

How Can We Get the Best out of the Four Factors?

Firstly, the four factors by themselves bring more joy to life. Therefore, don't assign them just to be used with the four tools. Make your awareness of them a part of your everyday life.

Secondly, having a good grasp on each of the four factors heightens our awareness of them. Here are some suggestions on how to get the best out of the four factors, which will in turn raise your awareness of them.

Make the relationship real: This is vital. The more the relationship touches your heart, the better. In personal relationships, we turn to each other for nourishment, support, love, friendship, assistance and intimacy. We are there for each other in good times and bad.

These same concepts need to be applied to our higher relationship. How can we do this? Here are some things I do to ensure that this relationship plays a 'real' part in my life.

As I work, chat and generally go about my day, in my mind I share my joys and sorrows with the energy of life. Throughout the day I ask for guidance and help whenever I need it and express my thanks and feelings of love for the support that comes to hand. This is particularly true when I work with clients. Throughout our session, inwardly I ask for higher direction and it's amazing what comes to light.

I think of the relationship especially when I'm helping someone, and when I'm listening to music, dancing, exercising, laughing or reading inspirational material. I see the energy of life as my friend and confidant who I can truthfully talk to without fear and judgement.

Every day I ask the energy of life questions; lots of them and then I look for answers. And throughout the day I give love and feel joy as much as possible. I do these things knowing that the energy of life is sensing, feeling and responding to my thoughts and feelings of genuine love. And at night I will often meditate. Sometimes I only manage a few brief minutes of meditation but those minutes are enough for me to feel the love and connection that exists between us.

I see my relationship with the energy of life as *the greatest one* in my life. It's the one I turn to most often for it's the one that steers me in the right direction and fills me with love, gratitude and joy.

I share this with you to help you understand that the basis for developing an intimate relationship is to connect heart to heart. To be aware of, think about, have fun with, turn to, talk to and *enjoy* the relationship that you have with the energy of life. The more awakened you are to the inseparable partnership that exists, the greater your joy will be.

Extra Tip. One way of remembering the importance of the relationship is to wear a ring. The ring serves two purposes. Firstly it's symbolic of union between you and the energy of life. Secondly, it serves as a physical reminder that assists you in remembering the importance of this higher relationship. Just by looking at the ring, it can remind you to turn to your higher relationship for help or it can remind you to thank the energy of life for an enjoyable moment that you have experienced.

Look for oneness: To make oneness real, we must look beyond viewing ourselves as individuals. We need to see the connection we have to each other and to the thread of life.

You can do this by creating and reflecting on thoughts that remind you that *one energy* connects everything together. Think about the following words: one life force; connection; unity; togetherness; wholeness; one source; one consciousness; one world; and one love. In your mind, reinforce the principle of oneness.

Use imagery to help you. For example, bring to mind the image that I mentioned earlier in the book—the strand being pulled from the bowl of spaghetti. Or create images that remind you that we are one. Creative visualisations are a great way of reinforcing the common thread we hold.

Turn to music as a source to remind you. I often listen to John Lennon's song "Imagine" as a piece of music that inspires and reminds me of the magic that oneness can bring to our lives.

Another oneness-enhancer is to spend time in nature. When we are entranced in the wonders of nature, we see that from the tiniest of insects to the mountains high, one energy source sustains all.

Expand your horizon, and allow the vision of oneness to permeate your world.

Love, love, love: Nothing makes us feel better than when we increase our ability to love.

In every aspect of our lives, we need to apply love not only to the people we love but to all of humanity. We need to love ourselves right now and in any given moment. We need to apply love to our studies, our careers, our finances and our life experiences—inclusive of our joys and sorrows.

Love has so many transformational qualities. I liken love's power to the transformation that occurs when you turn a light on in a darkened room. Even the tiniest bit of light has the power to reduce the darkness.

In the same way, love can reduce the negativity within us. It can cut the time we spend locked in the darkness of negative thoughts and feelings.

A quick way to raise yourself into the energy of love is to revisit your list of joys and read the "feelings that bring me inner joy" list. These feelings develop not only joy but love too. When you do activities to ignite these feelings, you raise yourself into the energies of love and joy. Both these energies are intrinsically entwined.

Improve your life by finding ways to power it with love.

Value energy: Everything stems from, is, exists in, and is supported by energy. There is so much information now in both the scientific and philosophic arenas that support these views. Make the effort to learn about these things, particularly the laws of attraction and the governing forces of life. They exist.

This knowledge will help you understand the principles behind the four tools and the four factors, and they will also enhance the way you use the tools and factors.

The great news is that "relationship," "oneness" and "love" ensure that you make the best use of *energy,* just as the four tools do too!

Everything that we are doing and learning about is designed to work positively with the principles of energy. So, if you practise what you have learned, you will maximise the power of energy. This will apply even if you don't fully understand the principles at work. Excellent!

In conclusion, let me reiterate an important point about the four factors—their power lies in your *awareness* of them. They are the energy of thoughts and feelings that ultimately result in higher actions.

The Reward

When you see the positive changes that occur in your life as a result of using the four tools and four factors, you will feel rewarded.

When you look back on a situation and see how quickly you were able to resolve it and how much better you feel for having done so, you just want to scream to the world, "Yes! I handled it in an empowering way!" The good feelings give you such a high!

Our ego-driven responses weigh heavily on our wellbeing. Lessening their power means living with more verve and joy.

Combined, the four tools and four factors take you on the high road to joy. They are your lifeline—the key practices to apply when things are not working in your life and when you want to enhance the good times you are experiencing.

The following chapters offer extra suggestions that help keep joy palpable in your daily life. These suggestions do not replace the four tools and four factors. They simply deliver more strategies to keep the abundance flowing. You can add many of the forthcoming tips to your list of joys.

Keys to the Abundance

- It is essential that, as you apply the four tools, you keep the awareness of the four factors at the forefront of your consciousness.
- ROLE power—the power source for the four tools.
- It's important to apply the understandings of the four factors not just to the four tools but to the everyday dealings of your life.

"Do not despair. When times are difficult do not allow your emotions to overwhelm you. Try to remain calm by focusing on the power of The Universe. Call upon It to help you. Ask It to solve the situation for you.

Many of you carry your burdens alone. You forget that you are entwined with the Universal Energy— that your relationship with It is inseparable. Call upon It to help you and you will be amazed at the miracles that appear in your life."

—Words from Spirit

PART IV

MORE TIPS TO LIVING
LIFE WITH JOY

There is no greater purpose than to love.
There is no greater happiness than joy.
Love and joy—virtuous virtues.
Cultivate them and fill your life with these two energies.

CHAPTER 15

HELPFUL QUESTIONS TO ASK WHEN THE GOING GETS TOUGH

"All things in life are presented to you so you can decide how to make the most of them. Even difficult situations are a gift, for they create the opportunity for growth."

—Words from Spirit

How our thoughts run wild during difficult times. I know when difficulties are present in my life it's a challenge to calm my mind. A practice that helps me to regain focus during these times is to engage in the exercise of "self-questioning." Self-questioning is an effective technique that breaks repetitive thought patterns by changing our focus of attention.

Here are four questions that I regularly ask myself when negative events take me down. You may like to ponder them the next time your thoughts and emotions lead you astray.

The Four Questions

1. What's causing my negative thoughts?

I ask myself, why am I feeling this way? For example, am I angry about a situation? Am I annoyed because my expectations have not been met? Am I feeling frustrated with myself or with someone else? Or am I feeling this way because I'm tired and just not thinking clearly?

There can be many reasons for our negative thoughts, and it's good to try to identify the reasons behind them.

2. Where are my thoughts directing my energy, attention, and focus?

I look at where are my thoughts are leading me. Are they guiding me in a positive or negative direction? If negative, then I ask myself if this is where I want to invest my personal energy and vitality.

3. Do I want to improve my thoughts and feelings?

This question is the one that really forces me to stop and think. It demands an answer—yes or no?

When my response to this question is yes, then the fourth question naturally flows.

4. What can I do to achieve this?

This question becomes a reminder to me that action is needed in order to change my thoughts and patterns of behaviour.

In troubled times, asking yourself these four questions will help redirect your energy, attention and focus. And once your focus has lifted, wow, it's so much easier to draw on resources that channel your energy in higher ways—the four tools and four factors being the perfect examples of great resources.

Next time your mind is giving you grief, give the four questions a go. Ask yourself:

- What's causing my negative thoughts?
- Where are my thoughts directing my energy, attention and focus?
- Do I want to improve my thoughts and feelings?
- What can I do to achieve this?

They are useful questions that will help steer you towards better outcomes.

Sometimes all it takes is a little change of direction to help us get back on track!

Extending the Power of Questioning

The big issues in life (i.e. relationships, health and finances) can deliver great joy as well as grief. Challenging times in any one of these areas can cause our joy level to plummet.

And the long-term effect of not dealing with the big issues in our life is that they can take our joy level down for extended periods of time—sometimes months or even years. This can affect our health and rob us of time that could have been better spent enjoying life.

So to lessen "down" time, here are some thought-provoking questions that encourage self-direction and positive action.

For ease of use, you can download these questions from my website.

Relationship Issues

Whether they are personal or work-related issues, ask yourself the following questions:

- When I rehash the negative thoughts over and over again in my mind, do these thoughts make me feel good? Do they make me feel better?
- Am I constantly blaming the other person?
- Are my thoughts hurtful towards the other person and towards myself? If so, do I want to invest my personal energy in these lower vibrations?
- What is my part to play in this situation?
- What action can I take that is in harmony with my spirit-self?
- What can I do to return to the feeling of joy?
- Every person who crosses my path is teaching me to love. What can I do in this situation to change the way I think and feel so that I am able to love in higher ways?
- What I think about others and how others make me feel—ultimately is energy that I'm attracting to my life! How can I improve my thoughts and feelings towards others so that I am attracting loving energy?
- Have I called on the four tools and four factors to help me during this time?
  Create your own questions below:

_____

_____

Health Issues

When you find yourself deep in worry about a health issue that you are experiencing, ask yourself these questions:

- Are my worrisome thoughts helping me to feel better or are they making my condition worse?
- Does my health improve when I'm focused on the negative outcomes of this particular illness?
- When I think and feel negatively, the feelings affect my cells. When I think and feel positively, these thoughts nourish my cells. What energy do I want to feed my cells—positive or negative?
- What can I do physically, emotionally, mentally and spiritually to help myself during this illness?
- What actions can I take in order to bring more joy-filled feelings to my life?
- There are many organs in my body that, in spite of my illness, are working well in order to keep me alive. Am I honouring and loving them? Am I honouring and loving my body, thanking it for all of its tireless work?
- Have I called on the four tools and four factors to help me find joy? Doing so will help to improve the way that I feel.

Create your own questions below:

_____

_____

Improving the Medical Care that You Are Receiving

Sometimes when undergoing medical treatments, we are not in the best frame of mind. Here are some questions that can raise personal energy levels and improve our outlook:

- Appreciation brings joy. Am I expressing gratitude to the health professionals, family members and people in my life who are helping me to get better?
- How can I help to make the treatments that I am receiving more successful? Could complementary therapies, such as Reiki or creative visualisation, improve my wellbeing during this time?
- There are so many simple joys that surround me each day (e.g. nature, children, random acts of kindness, etc.). Am I witnessing and noticing them?
- What can I do so that I focus less on my illness and more on the joys in my life?
- Have I called on the four tools and four factors to raise my sense of wellbeing?
  Create your own questions below:

_____

_____

Financial Issues

Financial stability is a common worry. Here are some questions that are worthy of reflection:

- Do my finances improve when I incessantly worry about them?

- Am I blocking myself from attracting abundance to my life by constantly focusing on "what I lack" as opposed to "what I have?"
- Am I witnessing grace in my life?
- Do I see and appreciate the abundance that is already in my life?
- Am I equating money with happiness?
- Do I really need more finances to support my situation, and if so, am I using my thoughts and feelings in positive ways to co-create abundance?
- Have I set the intention for opportunities to unfold that will help improve my finances?
- What can I do to help restore joy to my being so that my focus becomes less on worry and more on creating financial stability in a positive way?
- Am I prepared to handle this financial issue from higher thinking and with joy?
- What financial assistance can I give to others—even during the times when my budget is tight?
- The energy of life is responding to the focus of my energy and attention. Am I in "lack" mode, or am I in "gratitude" mode, thanking life for things great and small?
- Have I applied the principles of the four tools and the four factors to my life, which will improve my focus, energy, and attention during this time?
  Create your own questions below:

_____

_____

As you work through the questions, take note of the responses that come forth. There are times in our lives when we answer questions positively only to find that moments later self-sabotaging thoughts surface, thoughts that are unhelpful and that prevent us from taking positive action towards self-improvement.

So often our thoughts undermine our good intentions. This is because our ego-self tells us to fear. It feeds us excuses about why we can't change. It raises self-doubt. We are capable of more than what our ego-self tells.

The technique of self-questioning is a good way of letting the voice of our spirit-self rise above the noise of our ego. When our thoughts and feelings are low, we can break the cycle by asking and reflecting on some of the suggested questions.

Today is precious. Don't let old wounds of yesterday inflict pain on today. Instead, work on healing your issues so that you can get back to living life with joy.

Keys to the Abundance

- When negative events take you down, you can improve your focus of attention by asking yourself the 'four questions.'
- Self-questioning is a useful technique that helps to break repetitive negative thought patterns.
- In dealing with problems related to the big issues in life like relationships, health and finances, engage in self-questioning.

"Contained within every situation that you encounter is the choice of how you wish to manage that situation. Ultimately the power rests with you in how you wish to respond to the episodes of your life.

Your life-line of management, your guidance system that will lead you to the most appropriate way in which to respond is within you—your spirit.

If you choose to be directed by this guidance system your responses will be in harmony with life and for the betterment of your personal development.

Live life wisely. Make your choices in consultation with your spirit."

—Words from Spirit

CHAPTER 16

THE MEDICINAL POWERS OF JOY

"Don't take the path of life too seriously.
Remember enjoyment of life is heightened
when there is love and laughter."

—Words from Spirit

There is nothing better than a good laugh. Laughter—faster than anything else—lifts us into the vibration of joy. And the energy of joy benefits our bodies immensely. It helps us to live full and healthy lives.

The Effects Joy Has on Our Bodies

Our bodies are made up of trillions and trillions of cells. Cells are living energy, and they form our body tissues, vessels and organs.

Everything we think, feel, say and do affects the cells in our bodies and their health. We know this to be true because research confirms that our emotional state directly affects our immune, gastrointestinal, cardiovascular and respiratory systems. It alters our sleep patterns, energy levels and state of peace.

Constant stress, for example, leads to high blood pressure, and if left untreated, it can lead to kidney disease. We often get the flu or have flulike symptoms when we are stressed or run-down.

Your body cells are responding to and being affected by every stress in your body, especially emotional stress.

It is not possible for you to hold negative energy in your body daily without that energy affecting the health and vitality of your cells.

This is an important point to consider. All the grievances we harbour, the lack of love that we apply to our lives, the guilt we hold, and the blame we lay, all these things affect the building blocks of our bodies—our cells. Every bit of stress you hold touches your cells.

What Can We Do to Improve the Environment that Our Cells Live in?

Live with more joy. Joy is a natural cell-enhancer. When it's present in our lives, joy raises our vitality and injects good energy into our cells.

We have already learned of means that can help us live with more joy. The four tools, for instance, remind us that when we are more aware of our thoughts and feelings, we can take positive action towards thinking, feeling and doing things that make us feel better. This results in less stress, and less stress means a better environment in which our body cells exist.

The four factors, through keeping our thoughts and feelings aligned with our spirit-self, promote harmonious feelings. These joyous feelings improve our wellbeing.

Even with regard to our health, the four tools and four factors are beneficial, for they assist us to engage in practices that cultivate joy. This, in turn, has a positive effect on our health and wellbeing.

What else can we do?

Develop "Eyes of Appreciation" for Our Bodies

Many of us hold unhealthy views about our personal body image. We don't like our bodies because they're too fat, thin, short, tall or old. The shape of them is wrong, or the parts on them are too big, too small or too dangly!

Your body is the most amazing machine in the universe! Yes, it is! It tirelessly works twenty four hours a day, seven days a week to keep you alive. It always strives to maintain homeostatic balance, and it does this without any instruction from you!

How would you like to work so hard and not be acknowledged for your tireless, hard-working efforts?

One point that I stress time and time again to my clients is the importance of thanking their bodies daily. This act of appreciation develops feelings of self-love and it creates a less stressful environment for the body cells to replicate in and exist.

You can appreciate your body in simple ways. You can think about some of the major organs like the brain, liver, lungs, kidneys and heart and individually thank them for doing such an amazing job. Or, you can take a more general approach and thank your body organs and cells for all of the work that they do.

If some of your organs aren't functioning as well as you want them to, it is important that you feel compassion for those organs too. This will result in you holding higher feelings. Your unconditional love is more beneficial to your state of wellbeing than the vibrational energies of dislike and anger.

When you turn your attention away from what you don't like about your body and turn to loving your body, you feel much better. Try the following body-loving exercise.

Shower Exercise

Next time you bathe, as you rub the soap over your body, thank each part of your body. Thank your arms, legs, back, the organs within your body, your veins, arteries and capillaries. Go crazy! Thank every part of your body. Thanking your body is a feel good exercise.

It doesn't matter what shape your body's in. Your body is still amazing. It's amazing because no matter what's going on in your world, it's working 24/7 in an effort to keep you alive.

Unconditional love and appreciation of your body creates a joy-filled environment for the two million red blood cells that are created in your bone marrow every single second that you breathe!

Feeling Unwell? How Can Joy Help You Feel Better?

Whilst it can be particularly difficult during illness to maintain a positive outlook, it is essential that we try to do so. A happy mood speeds up our body's natural healing processes. Small changes can make a big difference to how we feel and manage our illnesses.

Here are six joy-enhancing tips that can help you when you are feeling unwell.

1. Improve your environment. Use colour, flowers, scents, art works or special photos to make the place where you are recuperating a nicer place to be. This may seem like such a simple act, but our environment greatly affects how we feel.

   Angela, our late relative, was confined to hospital for sixteen weeks. In her hospital room, there was a photo of her recent trip to Greece. She would look at the photo several times a day. The photo conjured great memories and feelings of joy within her, and she took delight in reflecting on the image. She also used the photo as a trigger to count the blessings in her life.

   Few I know would have been able to endure the many health complications Angela experienced whilst in hospital at that time. Her visioning, remembering, and recalling the joys in her life (Greece) and future joys (a niece's wedding) were driving forces that kept her in a positive frame of mind despite the serious illness that she was dealing with. As a result of her positive approach, she made it to the family wedding.

Make your room your castle. Fill it with your favourite things, and in doing so, you can bring joy to your heart and health.

2. Use affirmations. A good way to focus on getting better is to recite affirmations. For example, you can say, "I thank my body for the healing that is occurring now," or, "Every day, my body is helping me to get better and better." As you say the affirmation, check your feelings. It's essential that the feelings you charge the affirmation with, are as positive as the affirmation itself. (Otherwise, its beneficial effects will be negated).

    Affirmations are a great way of pushing aside negative thoughts and promoting healthy feelings. They are powerful because they improve our outlook, which in turn improves the energy that we feed the cells of our bodies.

3. Use signage. Place messages within your hospital room and/or your home that are uplifting. For instance, statements like "Positive-thought zone," "Healing room," and "Healing sanctuary" are great reminders about where you wish to direct your personal energy. Also, they give a clear message to others that you want to manage your illness in positive ways. When they see your attitude towards your illness, they are more likely to support your positive frame of mind.

4. Give gratitude. Show your appreciation to all who care for you, be they health professionals, family or friends.

    Holding an ungrateful, grumpy or arrogant attitude towards those who are helping you makes you feel worse, plus, your negative energy affects the energy levels of those caring for you. (Remember that it's all an energy exchange. The energy patterns you give out—others sense and feel). On the other hand, when you show appreciation towards those who care for you, they will enjoy looking after you!

So, be thankful to those who help you. You may not like being helped—because you may want to be independent—but whilst help is needed, be appreciative of it. You'll feel so much better in doing so, and your helpers will be uplifted by your loving attitude.

5. Use creative visualisation or guided imagery. If you haven't tried creative visualisation, I recommend that you do, for its uses are wide and varied. It will help you sleep better. It will settle your mind by using imagery to help you let go of negative thinking. It will allow you to feel more peaceful. Imagery is a powerful tool to help us deal with pain, boredom and fear.

   There are many books on creative visualisation that are helpful. Alternatively, you can purchase my *Power Your Healing* CD/MP3 (visit my website for more details), which will give you insight into how to help your body heal as well as provide you with a visualisation that relaxes you so that you can improve the state of your health. The visualisation is designed to help improve your recovery rate.

6. Play music. Music lifts our spirits and has a positive effect on our heart. I recommend that while you are recovering in hospital and staying at home, you designate a time each day when you "chill out" and listen to relaxing music. Take your mind off yourself for a while, get lost in music, and feel how it both raises and touches you deeply.

You can also watch DVDs that combine music with images of nature. Restful DVDs, especially ones that use guided imagery, can help relax your body. Once again, I recommend using this tool daily.

Allow the Vibration of Joy to Improve Your Health!

To improve your general health and/or to speed up your recovery from an illness, adopt joy as a healing strategy. The nature of joy is that it gives your body permission to heal.

More often than not, we don't allow our body to heal. When the body is constantly being fed information that reinforces that it is ill, recovery becomes slower and harder for the body. This is because the cells in the body are being affected by, and responding to, the negative thoughts and feelings that we hold.

It takes much longer to get over sicknesses when you hold bad feelings towards your body. It's better to *help* your body and assist it in its ability to heal by adopting practices that raise your thoughts and feelings, ones that unearth the diverse qualities of joy.

Extra Tip: Turn to your list of "feelings that bring me inner-joy" and draw on those feelings while you are managing your illness. By using the four tools and four factors to help cultivate feelings of joy, you will develop a better approach to your health.

In Summary

Joy is one of the *best* energy sources to feed the cells of your body.

When recovering from illness or surgery, apply the six tips. If you have a chronic, long-term condition, I recommend that you put the six tips plus ideas that come to you on a separate list entitled "better health through joy." Refer to this list when you want to improve your medical condition and your attitude towards it.

Our body is not permanent. At some point, our body will cease to be. It is important that whilst we have a body, we appreciate it and help it by holding positive feelings and attitudes.

If illness is part of our life script, then we can use the energy of joy to help improve how we feel. We may not always be able to cure our illness. We may not be able to change what has happened to our body, but we can change how we think, feel, and manage our health.

Joy helps us to manage our health in more productive ways.

Some say laughter is the best medicine. I say it's *joy!*

Keys to the Abundance

- Joy has a positive effect on the health of your cells. By lessening stress in your life and in holding more joy, you create a better environment for your body cells.
- During times of ill health, apply the six tips to improve recovery.
- Thanking your body and holding a positive attitude towards it is a health-enhancing step.

"We ask you to nourish your body with good thoughts. It works continuously and tirelessly for you, therefore, we ask you to respect it by acknowledging it, thanking it, and honouring it for all that it does to maintain your physical existence.

Your body is the vehicle that carries you over the terrain of life. Look after it well and nourish it with love and loving thoughts."

—*Words from Spirit*

CHAPTER 17

JOY AT WORK

*"Work with enthusiasm. You spend a
great deal of your waking hours being
employed or managing your personal
business. Enjoy the work that you do."*

—Words from Spirit

On average, a third of your life is spent at work, so it makes
sense to enjoy your working life. When you don't enjoy your
occupation, you unconsciously hold dissatisfied feelings for
several hours each day. These feelings are neither healthy to
your body nor uplifting to your soul.

What can we do to improve job satisfaction? Here are some
tips on how you can gain more joy from work.

Seven Ways to Inject Joy into Your Working Life

1. *At the end of each day, reflect on the positives.* Make
    a note of the kind actions that you engaged in. For
    example, you may have gone out of your way to help a
    client or customer. You may have spent time assisting a
    colleague. Perhaps you took a stance against your ego

and chose to be polite to someone instead of blowing your fuse! Yes, that's worth acknowledging. Feel good about the small kindnesses that you deliver as you work.

Also, feel good about the problems you solved or the decisions you made that resulted in good outcomes.

Often our focus is placed on the negative aspects of the day—the angry client, the dissatisfied customer, the annoying boss or bad employee. Switch your attention so that your energy is focused on positive aspects. Kind actions and positive outcomes are food for your soul.

2. *Do your best.* There is nothing more satisfying than knowing that at the end of your working day, you have put in your best effort. Doing your best is a good motto to work by. It brings personal satisfaction. It means you are an asset to the companies that you work for. It engenders respectful feelings towards your colleagues and it fosters good feelings.

Extra tip: A good technique to use when your working day is not going so well is to change your focus. Instead of holding thoughts that reinforce the bad day that you're having, change your thoughts to centre on this statement: "I'm giving this day my best." By approaching it in this manner, you'll be less caught up in the drama of the day and more focused on making the best of the situation.

A lot of joy flows when we give the working day our best.

3. *Bless your day.* Think about how you view your work. Do you see it as a chore, a way to earn bread and butter, or a duty that you have to fulfill? Do you feel that you

work out of "necessity" as opposed to viewing work as an interesting part of your life? If you have answered yes to any of these, then try the following techniques.

You can stop the workday blues by setting the intention of gratitude. When you wake up in the morning, bless the day ahead. Affirm the following statements: "I bless all with whom I work today. Everyone I meet I bless. I am blessed to be able to work, to have a job, to be employed. My life is blessed, and I bless my work!"

As you get ready for work, affirm your good qualities and those of the people with whom you work. Focusing on the positive qualities in yourself and others is a better approach to the day than going over the negatives.

Holding an attitude of being happy to go to work is important. If you are projecting energy in thought forms and feelings that say, "My work is a chore," then you are saying to the energy of life, "Make this day a chore!" You are feeding your body, mind and spirit vibrations that are low and dreary.

You can change your attitude towards work and bring more joy to your life by blessing everyone in your day and by being appreciative of the fact that you are fit enough, healthy enough and lucky enough to have a job. Sure, right now it may not be your dream job, but when you hold better thoughts and feelings towards your work, you allow better opportunities to come your way.

For now, bless your life, your work, and everyone associated with your work. Holding kind attitudes brings joy.

Extra tip: When you enter your workplace building, send out a thought, "I bless this building and everyone who works within it." Spreading joy and blessings to all is a loving and uplifting gesture.

4. *Honour your values.* My life focus is to help others, and this is a personal value that I am very clear about as I work. It's what drives me to do what I do. Consequently, when I honour this value, I feel joy.

   What values are you passionate about? Are you applying them to your working life, or are your values sitting on the back burner because you're too caught up in the worldly aspects of your job?

   Our personal values foster joy. They bring worth to our working lives. When we disregard our personal values, we feel dissatisfied. When we follow them, we feel joy stemming from our deeper self.

   Extra tip: Ensure your personal values are featured in your list of inner joys. They are important to your wellbeing. Joy will exude from you when you follow them.

5. *Morale is important.* Become a morale booster at work. Compliment colleagues on the good work that they do or let them know that you appreciate their skills. Be cheerful and let your demeanour raise the spirits of others. Spreading joy at work is infectious. When you spread happiness, the joy that you give to others uplifts you too.

   And if you are self-employed, it doesn't hurt to boost your own morale every now and then. It's good to acknowledge that your hard-working efforts contribute to society and that the work you do makes a difference. This little act of self-love will perk you up for the day.

Extra tip: Why not make Monday "Morale Day" by boosting morale in your workplace. Begin the working week on a positive note.

6. *Look at what really drives you.* What brings you joy as you work? Is it being with your work colleagues or being part of a team? Is it providing great customer service? Is it the sheer love of the work that you do? Is it the challenge of using your mind? Is it because you can be creative or you help people or you're competent and confident at what you do?

   Discover the qualities that you love about your occupation. Reflecting on these qualities is energising. When you feel good about the work that you do, you energetically attract positive experiences to you.

7. *Appreciate your pay.* When you receive payment for services rendered, shriek with joy—inside and out. Thank the energy of life for the sum of money that has been given to you. This gesture says to the energy of life that you are thankful for the money that comes into your life. It fosters a multiplicity of money.

   So many people, once they receive their pay packet, focus on the bills that need to be paid and the lack of money that they have, or they express a desire for more pay, more money. They're unaware of the first rule towards increasing financial abundance, specifically *appreciation*. When money comes your way—whether the amount is large or small—feel grateful for the sum. Honour the energy of money that has come into your hands, and the energy of life will honour you with more money!

Extra tip: If you want to increase your financial abundance or you are hunting for a pay rise, practise this technique: Each time you receive money, exclaim to yourself, "Wow!" Really feel the joy of having that money and thank the energy of life for the gift it has given you. Then, with joy in your heart, say to the energy of life, "I joyfully receive money, and I am open to receiving more of it!" Say this over and over again. As you pay your bills, affirm this statement. Feel good about paying bills and feel good about receiving money in your life. Open your ability to create more and receive more through appreciation and gratitude.

What to Do if You Are Unhappy with Your Job

The last thing you want to do to yourself is go through life with unhappy thoughts and feelings when it comes to your job. If you don't like your job, then it's time to do something about it!

The first step towards changing your circumstances requires that you be honest with yourself. You see, many times we blame our bosses or work colleagues as the reason for disliking our job. But often the truth of the matter is that we're unhappy because the job is not meeting our inner needs. Others become the excuse for our dissatisfaction. They are not the cause of this feeling.

When we hold an attitude in relation to our job that says, "It's a job, and it earns the dollars," or "I'm not happy with my job, but it's the only work that I know how to do," we create problems for ourselves.

If you believe that it's the only job that you can do or that you're "trapped" in the job, then you will stay stuck there. Why? Because your energy (in the form of your thoughts and feelings) is saying to the energy of life, "Hold me here because this is it, this is all I can do."

To shift out of this thought pattern, you first must acknowledge how you are truly feeling (trapped and unhappy) and then use the four tools and four factors to lift your feelings back into the energy of joy. Sometimes all it takes is a change in attitude to bring about job satisfaction.

Other times, however, we discover that although we have improved our attitude, we're unhappy with our job on a deeper level. If this turns out to be the case, then here is how to put forth the intention for change.

How to Set Your Intention for Change

Your intention for change begins by planting thoughts and feelings that a better job is available for you. You *don't have to figure out how that is going to happen*. You simply put the thought out there so that the energy of life hears, "There's a great job that's just right for *me!*"

Then improve your personal energy by applying the seven tips that I have just given you as well as the four tools and four factors to your current job. This is vital. Things won't improve until you change your attitude.

Don't get caught thinking that once you have the "perfect job," then you'll change your thoughts and feelings. No! You have to inject joy into the current job that you hold. Once you start to lift yourself into the energy of joy, *then* the energy of life will respond positively to your energy shift, and things will begin to change in a positive direction.

So it's important to be honest when it comes to how you feel about the work you do. Once you're aware of how you are feeling, you can stop self-sabotaging thoughts and feelings by calling on joy to help you create better experiences in your life.

Remember, when you choose to make positive changes to your life, the energy of life *supports* your choice.

Using Your Lifeline—The Four Tools and Four Factors

As mentioned, you can use the four tools to help you get more enjoyment from your occupation. To do this, determine whether your thoughts towards your employment are primarily positive or negative.

Feel what is going on inside of you and learn the truth of how you feel about your working life. Now that you have the full picture, use the fourth tool to improve your thoughts and feelings.

If your thoughts and feelings are predominantly positive in relation to your work, see if you can incorporate some of the practices from your list of joys to further spark job satisfaction. The aim is to keep the energy of joy alive and palpable.

If your thoughts and feelings are not positive, then your first move is to use your list and engage in activities that uplift you.

You are more likely to make changes and stay committed to change when you first improve your feelings. Once you feel better, you have more energy to apply positive strategies to your life.

Going over negative thoughts and feelings in our head and heart depletes joy. Taking action is the key. Lifting how we are feeling and desiring good feelings promotes action.

Are You Tired?

Sometimes it isn't the nature of the work that we do or the people we work with that is the problem. Sometimes it's simply that we are physically tired and that our physical fatigue lessens our enjoyment of work.

If you have been working too hard lately, elements on your list of joys will remind you that rest is important, along with activities that boost your energy levels. Your productivity increases when you feel better within yourself.

Our work life has an impact on our health and wellbeing. While it may not be practical to suddenly change our job, it is practical to change our *attitude and feelings* towards our work. Not to change this lessens our enjoyment of life.

How the Four Factors Improve Working Life

Greater insight influences your responses in positive ways.

Relationship builds trust, trust that the right job will come your way, trust that your work problems will get solved. In relationship, you feel supported by a higher source that can help you.

Through oneness, you see the link you have with all the people you work with. Everyone is part of a team working towards a common goal, and that common goal can only be reached by the sum of many working as one.

Love influences how you work. It directs you towards being honest, respectful, and kind to others, with a desire to help others and work to the best of your ability. As love motivates your work, the enjoyment you get from your occupation increases. Also, love places your personal energy in a different realm. It lessens the focus on working for "the dollars" and increases attention on working towards doing your best or making a difference in someone's life. Job satisfaction is born out of these values.

And energy reminds you that it's your role to attract better circumstances to your working life by being conscious of the energy of life and working with it in positive ways.

The Ego's Work Habits

The ego likes to engage in judging others. In particular, when we have an issue with someone at work, our ego focuses our attention on the negative attributes of the other person. It will tell us that the person is inflexible, inept, lazy, not skilled enough, etc.

While there may be some truth in the comments made by the ego, the fact is that we can't always change our bosses or our work colleagues. People don't always behave in the ways we want or expect them to. There are times in our career when dealing with people in the work place is challenging. During these times it's best to manage the situation by focusing our attention on strategies that are helpful.

The seven strategies, the four tools and the four factors pave the way towards a better approach. They improve our level of job satisfaction, and they give us strength to make career decisions that are not always easy. And most importantly, they make us feel better. When we are feeling better, *then* we are able to make better life choices.

Keys to the Abundance

- A happy working life makes life more enjoyable.
- The seven tips help to lessen work dissatisfaction and increase work satisfaction.
- Injecting joy into your current job position is important because it creates positive energy that attracts positive circumstances to your life.

"Bring passion to your work. Feel enthusiasm for all that you do. Put the right energy into your activities. These are some of the ways in which you can bring more joy to your life.

The way you approach things makes a difference to your experience of them."

—Words from Spirit

CHAPTER 18

HOLDING ON TO JOY

*"Just for today be positive. To all the episodes
that unfold in your day, respond with positive
thoughts and actions. Just for today let go of
negative attitudes and feelings. Let go of things
that annoy and disturb you. Just for today be
happy with your lot. Be content knowing that
you will always be loved and taken care of.*

*Just for today let go of your troubled mind
and see the blessings in your life."*

—Words from Spirit

I take comfort in the phrase, "Just for today." Concentrating on one day at a time helps to curb thoughts that so eagerly want to jump to the future. There is so much joy to be had in savouring each day.

In addition to taking one day at a time, what other practices can we include that will help us stay joy-centred?

Practical Ways that Help Us Stay Focused

Here is a list that will help you to experience joy more often:

1. Keep focused on the positive events that occur in your day. Be attuned to the kind words and actions that you hear and see. Recognise the courtesies, the loving actions that touch your life, such as the times when someone pays for your coffee or when a person offers you his or her parking space. Set your sights on witnessing the kind acts that occur every day. This will uplift you and inspire you to higher action.

2. Surround your work and home environments with inspirational material. Display posters that have inspiring messages—pictures, photographs, and artworks that are uplifting. Place affirmations in front of your work area. And keep your favourite motivational books handy and nearby. Refer to them when you need pepping up. Enriching your environment with inspirational material—especially at work—helps to keep your energy positive.

3. Make time in your diary for *yourself*. Each week, schedule an appointment time with yourself and participate in something that brings you joy during the session. You may use the time for meditation, contemplation, reading inspiring material, or exercising. It doesn't matter how you use the time. What does matter is that you make an appointment each week with yourself!

   When the opportunity arises, block off a day and attend an uplifting seminar or workshop. Go on retreat. Treating yourself in inspiring ways helps to keep you feeling good and recharged. It may take courage to do these things, but you'll feel a whole lot better for doing them.

4. Keep music flowing through your life. It's a great way to lift your vibes! Play music while you are cooking or attending to daily chores. Allow the energy of music to energise you and change everyday routines into positive scenes!

5. Keep a journal. Each day, write about your joyful encounters. Document them so that you have evidence of the simple joys that touch your life each day. Something special occurs every day. Look for that event and make a note of it.

    Extra tip: Combine this practice with the first suggestion (witnessing kindnesses). In the evening, journal about your experiences. This daily review is evidence that many good things are taking place in your life.

6. Read and listen to inspirational material as often as you can. If you are stretched for time, listen to audios while you are driving the car or taking public transport. Read instead of watching television. Feed your mind, soul and senses with positive food.

7. Energise your thoughts by training your mind to think of joy more often. A great way to achieve this is to bring to mind the word "joy." Then mentally say, "I charge my thoughts with joy. I charge my thoughts with joy." Repeat this statement several times over and over again.

    As often as possible throughout the day, think and repeat the word "joy."

Extra tip: Set the alarm on your mobile phone to ring at set or random times throughout the day. When the alarm goes off, stop what you are thinking and say to yourself, "I charge my thoughts with joy." Feel good as you say and repeat this in your mind.

I applied this practice by setting the alarm on my phone to ring at 3:00 p.m. each day. Why then? There are three letters in the word "joy," and the three letters reminded me to think about joy at three o'clock. I don't need the alarm to remind me now. When it's 3:00 p.m., I'm in the habit of charging my thoughts with joy! It's a technique that reinforces the fact that joy is important to me.

8. Spend time with like-minded friends. Support, inspire and motivate each other. Good company will help to keep you focused and on track.

9. Dance, dance, dance. If you want an instant joy "fix," turn on the music and dance. Moving your body to music is energising, freeing and joy-enhancing. Be spontaneous. Grab your partner or your children and dance. Have some fun!

10. Keep on hand a collection of comical movies. There is nothing better than watching funny films and skits.

11. Take the challenge and commit to living each day one day at a time. Affirm, "Just for today, I am going to be happy. I am going to be worry-free and enjoy my life. Just for today, I am going to love life!"

When we begin the day in this frame of mind, we set the tone for how we want the day to unfold.

Extra tip: Why not place the above affirmation next to your bedside table. You can set the intention for your day by awakening to these positive words.

12. Spread the vibe of joy often. As I walk past passers-by, I look at them, and in my mind, I say to them with all sincerity, "I wish you endless joy." As I say the words, I feel them in my heart and I feel the inner excitement in wishing others joy. It's so energising when you love feeling joy so much that you just want to share it with everyone.

Try playing this little game and see how you feel when you secretly share and pass joy to others. It's more fun than walking around with worrying thoughts or reeling off shopping lists in your mind.

Joy is free, so share it freely!

The above practices contribute greatly to helping you stay uplifted and charged with joy. You may not be able to participate in all of them each day, but incorporating a few practices into your daily routine will help to keep you feeling good. Life's good when you're feeling good!

Look for the Proof that Joy Is Changing Your Life!

Often in my workshops, I stress the importance of looking for the everyday proof that you are in sync with the energy of life. This is essential because the more coincidences you see occurring in your life, the more evidence you have that confirms your newfound thinking is working for you. Confirmation brings joy.

How can you get into the habit of doing this?

Start your day by saying to the energy of life, "Today, give me evidence that you and I are manifesting positively." Then look for the signs. Witness the little things that occur daily. Doing this elevates your sense of joy.

I lead a busy life, and because of this, I have learned to rely on the energy of life to help me during my day. In my heart and mind I ask with joy for the help that I need, and I firmly believe that I will receive help. Then I look for the evidence. Every day, proof appears.

The energy of life helps me to shop. (I don't usually have a lot of time for shopping). It guides me to the right store at the right time to find exactly the things I need. Here are two more examples of how the energy of life has helped me with my every day needs.

On one occasion, I required some garden mulch, but I didn't have the time to drive to a garden centre to buy it. So I put the thought "out there," and within the hour, a man knocked on our front door. He was selling garden mulch!

A similar thing happened when we needed our tree to be lopped. I planted the thought "out there" for a tree-lopping firm to be in the neighbourhood. Later that day, a tree-lopping firm knocked on our front door. Our house number was written on the quote sheet instead of our neighbour's house number! I pointed them to the correct house and asked if they could attend to our tree. They did, and once again, my problem got sorted without me having to make a phone call!

Experiences like these occur often in my life. I believe they do because I am deliberate about directing my personal energy in such a way that I ask for them to occur, I want them to occur, and I look for them to happen in my life.

And best of all, when I am going through difficult times, I recall some of the magical coincidences that I have experienced in the past, and through the recollections, I can't help but smile and be reassured that I am not alone—help is on its way.

Every day, I look forward to seeing the proof in my day. Why don't you try doing this too? Set your intention and ask for help. And when you see the proof appearing in your life, make sure you acknowledge it, rejoice in it, and feed off it so that your joy level rises and you create the energy pattern for more of these magical moments to occur. (Remember to document them in your list of joys).

When you are conscious of your connection to the life force and look for the signs that your awareness is manifesting positively, joy abounds.

All of the suggestions within this chapter will help you to stay focused on joy. Incorporate some of the practices into your life, and you will find that you'll experience joy more often each day. If you find yourself out of sync with joy, return to this chapter. Adopting a few of the practices will quickly help raise your joy level again.

Keys to the Abundance

- It helps to stay focused on managing life one day at a time.
- Raise the fun level in your life every day.
- Each day, look for the proof that your joy-filled awareness is manifesting positive outcomes in your life.

"Begin the day in a positive way. Say upon rising, 'I will radiate joy to all whom I meet; I will enjoy my day.'

No matter your circumstance, face the day in a positive way and joy will fill your being."

—*Words from Spirit*

CHAPTER 19

GETTING RID OF NEGATIVE ENERGY

*"When another person's energy vibrations are
down it does not mean that you have to lower
your vibrations to match theirs. On the contrary!
Strive to rise above their negative vibrations
by holding your energy in the heart of joy."*

—*Words from Spirit*

So, you are feeling more joyful, but the people around you
are not. The media is not. Maybe your partner or children are
not. All of these situations have an effect on your personal
energy field.

As a walking, talking, thinking, feeling and creating mass
of vibrational energy, the people and the environment that
surrounds you affects you. Sometimes the effects of other
people's negativity on your body are felt instantly. For example,
listening to someone who is down can make you feel drained
in no time at all. Sometimes the effect can be subtle. You may
not be overtly aware of the cause. You may simply know that
something's up and you don't feel good.

What can you do to regain your power?

Here are some practices that you can apply at any time to improve your personal energy levels. These five techniques address some of the common negative experiences that we encounter daily and they will help you to become less affected by them.

The Breath of Life—Breathing Technique

This technique is good to use when someone else's energy affects you in a negative way (as in the case of negative conversations) or when you need a recharge (e.g., when you are feeling tired).

Find a quiet spot. While you are sitting or standing, take a deep breath in and then *quickly and forcibly* expel the breath. Do this three times in quick succession.

After the third time, pause and then take in *a relaxed breath*, releasing the outward breath gently and slowly. Do this three times, ensuring that the outward breath is released very slowly. When you have finished, remain still for a minute and enjoy the peaceful feelings. Now *smile*.

It takes less than two minutes to do this powerful recharging exercise. Smiling at the completion of the exercise is necessary. This action feeds positive information to your brain that encourages you to feel happy, peaceful and good. You can bring on a happy feeling simply by smiling.

Letting Go—Visualisation

This technique is good to use when mental worries are dragging you down. This visualisation is particularly useful during the times when your mind is burdened or when you have engaged in communications that have left you feeling gloomy. Whatever the cause of your heavy thoughts, this visualisation will help you let go of them.

Begin by sitting comfortably with your eyes closed, your hands on your lap, and your palms facing upwards. Now imagine that a receptacle, such as a basket, is placed in front of you. Visualise this basket and see yourself unloading all the worries of your mind into it—your fears, concerns, anxieties and frustrations. Place all of your worries into the basket along with the negative feelings that you are holding onto. It feels good to let go of these things.

Now see the basket slowly lift up in front of you. See it float away towards the blue sky. It drifts further and further away from you, gently floating off into the perfect sky.

Watch the basket disappear from your vision. It feels so good to see it disappear. For the next thirty seconds or so, enjoy the contented and freeing feelings that you experience now that you have released your burdens.

When you are ready, take in a gentle breath and then exhale slowly. Smile before you open your eyes.

This visualisation, which brings a sense of calmness and peace to your being, can be completed in less than two minutes.

If you are feeling tired or overwhelmed, if your mind is cluttered with worries or your joy measure is low, turn to this exercise for help. If worrying thoughts return later, simply recall this image. See your basket of troubles once again floating out of your life.

Body Protector—Visualisation

This technique is good to use when you want to protect yourself from absorbing negative energy projected by others, you want to lessen the effects of negative energy that you may have absorbed, or you want to keep your energy field healthy and in good shape. This visualisation can be done while you are sitting, standing or lying down. Whichever way you choose make sure your eyes are closed.

Imagine that you are standing inside an oval shape (like standing inside an egg). Now imagine that your arms are fully outstretched. This will give you the approximate distance that lies between your body and the oval line.

The inside area of the oval is your personal energy field. The oval line is your band of *protection.* It safeguards your energy field and protects you from negative forces.

In your imagination, fill your energy field (the area all around your body) with light. The warmth of the light feels good and nourishing to your body.

Now look at the oval band encasing you. See it as a rich golden colour. Watch it shimmer and glow. See your entire body fully enclosed and protected by this beautiful gold band. Held within it, you feel safe, secure and warm.

Hold this image for the next minute or so and enjoy the loving feelings that surface. When you are ready, *smile* and then slowly open your eyes.

This exercise is extremely useful in helping you strengthen and protect your energy field.

A note about the second and third exercises: If you're struggling to create the imagery, visit http://www.lightwords.com.au/audio on my website and download both visualisations. It's easier to master them if you are guided through them. Don't simply dismiss them because you think that the exercises are a little whacky!

Part of the power contained within these exercises is associated with the act of pausing. When we pause, we momentarily stop mental chatter and negative feelings. We bring peace to our body. The imagery created in both of these exercises is specifically designed to benefit your body, mind and spirit.

I encourage you to give them a try.

Colours of Life—Mood Lifter

This technique is good to use when you want to uplift the way you feel or improve your mood.

This is a very simple technique. Look at the colours of life surrounding you. Are you dressed in dark tones all the time? Take a look at the colours in your living environment. Are the colours in your home affecting you, making you feel low?

Can your office do with a splash of brightness? You can create this through a single flower, a colourful ornament, or a piece of artwork that uplifts you.

Studies show that colours affect our moods and feelings. They affect our level of vibrancy and sense of wellbeing. They have the power to change how we feel. So during the times when you're feeling down, look at what you can do to add a splash of colour to your day. Why not pick yourself some colourful flowers? Why not wear a snazzy shirt or tie? How about wearing a bright scarf or some coloured socks to work? Why not add a colourful and funky accessory?

Lift your day in a colourful way. Colours colour life!

Sensory Overload—Daily Self-protection

This technique is an exercise in self-awareness.

Are you in sensory overload? Are you addicted to watching or listening to the news? Are you surrounded by people whose conversations are predominately negative? Is the music that you listen to down on mood? What about the food you eat? How does it make you feel? Healthy, happy and energised or tired and listless? Think about these things because they affect you.

You are energy and everything you feed your senses through sight, sound, taste, smell and touch touches you. Therefore, it's important to take into account the whole picture and look at what you can do to reduce sensory overload in your life.

Could you, for example, watch less news reports or read the newspapers less frequently? I rarely watch the news or read newspapers, yet I still find out what's going on in the world. People inform me, or on a particular day, my intuition drives me to read the paper. I choose to allow important news to come to me—as opposed to me being immersed in news. This approach is worth a try.

There are other things that you can do to lessen sensory overload. Remove yourself from conversations that are foul-mouthed or negative. When people go on about "their issue," be that political, financial, and yes, even spiritual, when they beat their drum, or they express anger, simply remove yourself from their presence. If this is not possible, then do the body protection visualisation and surround yourself in a cocoon of light. Place your consciousness in the protection of love and joy.

As much as reasonably possible, avoid exposing yourself to outside influences that eat away at your vitality.

Add to Your List of Joys

Try the five techniques and see if some of them uplift you. If they do then add them to your list of joys in the category headed: "things I do to ignite the feelings of inner joy." This will help remind you of them and encourage you to use them when the need arises.

It's about Self-love

When negative energy affects our wellbeing, it's time to apply helpful strategies that release the negative effects.

Taking care of our personal energy field is *an act of self-love*. It helps us to stay more buoyant throughout the fluctuations of life. It keeps us in great shape.

Keys to the Abundance

- It's important to be mindful of, and to take care of your personal energy field.
- Other people's energy affects your state of wellbeing. Therefore, you need to apply strategies to your life that keep your personal energy vibes in good shape.
- Taking care of your personal energy field is an act of self-love.

"Negative emotional energy drains
the body and silences the spirit.

Therefore, learn to develop practices that protect
you from negative forces, ones that lift your
vibrations to those which are most compatible with
your body, mind and spirit—those of love and joy."

—Words from Spirit

CHAPTER 20

QUICK FIXES

*"In the stresses of the day, take time to rest.
Close your eyes; take some deep breaths
and let your mind drift into silence.*

*Two minutes of solitude in a busy
schedule can revive you and help you
to manage the rest of your day.*

*Communion and connection; these things are
important in removing stress from your day."*

—*Words from Spirit*

We all have days when we are feeling great and then something occurs that lessens our sense of joy. What things can we do to shift and lift our energy during these times?

I have created an action plan that offers quick joy-boosting solutions to help manage daily situations that arise. There are seven scenarios, and each one of them has one action you can employ.

These suggestions are *quick fixes* (as opposed to the four tools and four factors that offer long-term solutions). They have a primary purpose, and that is to lift your feelings in the moment. In raising your feelings, you become more productive and less affected by daily changes.

As you apply the quick fixes to your life, you may develop alternative strategies that work well for you. You can write your personal ideas in the "your suggestion" area under the appropriate heading.

Your bright and happy demeanor becomes affected by someone's negative attitude.

You feel this way because your energy field senses the other person's energy field. In sensing their lower vibrations, instead of protecting yourself from them, you allow your energy vibration to drop down and match the same vibrational energy of the other person.

What should you do? Do the "Breath of Life" exercise (from the previous chapter). Expelling the breath forcibly releases built-up tension in your body. At the completion of the exercise, jump up and down on the spot for a minute, lightly flicking your hands back and forth. Physical movement helps to re-energise the body.

Your aim is to lift your vibrations back to a level that makes you feel better. Why hold onto someone else's negative energy? Let the person hold onto this energy if he or she so wishes, but you take positive action that raises you out of the negative vibes.

Your suggestion: _____

_____

You are feeling flat and not joyful.

You may feel this way because you are surrounded by negative people in your home or workplace. You may be giving too much of yourself to others. Your mind could be burdened by the problems in your life. You may be physically tired.

What should you do? Carry out an act of self-love. For example, take time out for a walk. Have a nap, go for a swim, or do something nurturing just for you.

Why? Because when you express love towards yourself, you feel better. In feeling better, you then have the energy to cope with the many different things that occur in your day.

Your suggestion: _____

_____

You are experiencing a lacklustre day.

You may feel this way because you believe that your day is unrewarding. You may feel routines run your life. You may be bored feeling that your life just seems to be drifting on. Perhaps your energy levels are low.

What should you do? Perform a random act of kindness. Why? Because the best way to break away from the mundane is to reach out and help others. When you do something to uplift someone else (or improve the life of a bird or animal), your life gets a boost too! These acts help you to feel purposeful and useful, and they make the day worthwhile. There is nothing better than an act of kindness to add brightness to the day.

Your suggestion: _____

_____

The day delivers one "drama" after another.

This may be happening to you because you started the morning off by thinking that your day wouldn't go smoothly, and then it doesn't! It may well be just one of those days. Yep, they happen!

What should you do? Throughout the day, affirm the following: "Today, I will go with the flow. I will accept what is, knowing that everything occurs for a reason."

If you have a problem remembering the affirmation, write it on a note and carry the note with you. Better still, recite and write the affirmation. Give it your utmost attention.

Why? Some days are full of events. When we change our expectation about how the day *should* unfold and when we change our attitude towards the happenings that are going on and choose to go with the flow, we become less stressed and frustrated.

In the flow of life, nothing happens by chance. Every moment unfolds in accordance with our life plan. Reminding ourselves to accept the unfolding of the day helps us cope better.

Your suggestion: _____

_____

Physical tiredness stops you from feeling joy.

This may be happening to you because your thoughts are weighing you down. Your mind may be overstimulated. Perhaps you give of your time freely to others with little time for yourself. You may be working too hard. You may not be eating properly, or you have a busy home life.

What should you do? Get active. Go for a walk. Do yoga. Start dancing. Swim, jog or participate in physical activities that are appealing to you. Switch your mind off for a while and get active about lifting your energy.

Why? Because exercising energises your body. In truth, exercise is often the last thing that we feel like doing when we are tired, but it's the best cure when it comes to boosting our personal energy levels!

Your suggestion: _____

_____

You are in too much of a rush to feel joy.

This may be happening to you because you have too many things going on in your life. You may have overcommitted yourself for the day. You may be taking on other things in order to avoid something that you really don't want to do. You could be overworked and you may not have enough support from others to help you achieve what needs to be done.

What should you do? You need a "peace moment." Visit a park or stop what you are doing, go outside for a few moments and breathe in the fresh air. Go for a walk. Engage in a quick meditation technique. Turn to an inspirational book or a pack of inspirational cards and get an uplifting message for yourself.

Why? Because pausing for a while and participating in an act that brings peaceful feelings reduces stress levels. When your stress level is reduced, you function better.

Your mind may tell you that you don't have time to rest, but you have to be firm and ignore its unhelpful comments. Do something that allows you to experience peace. Realistically, if ten minutes is all that you can manage, ten minutes is better than nothing. These ten minutes will clear your mind and help you become more efficient when you are doing what you need to do.

Your suggestion: _____

_____

A sudden and unexpected happening completely throws your day.

Why does this happen? It's unavoidable. Life is not scripted exactly as we think it should be. Sudden illness occurs. Accidents happen. Expectations are broken. Relationship issues challenge us. In the unfolding of life, change is constant.

What should you do? Become present focused. A quick way to do this is to recite an affirmation. This will help direct your focus and attention. Here are some suggestions:

- "I easily adapt to the changes in my life."
- "I am strong. In my strength, I ask the energy of life for help, and help comes to me."

- "By taking one step at a time, I manage this situation effectively."
- "When my focus and attention is positive, I make better decisions."
- "I know that right now I can manage, adapt and adjust."

Why? Because when sudden changes occur, our mind becomes filled with troublesome thoughts. These thoughts only add to the stress we are dealing with at the time.

Affirmations help to calm our thoughts. Through them, we gain strength and direction. We regain personal power.

Your suggestion: _____

_____

Today Is Precious!

Our lives are better managed through the energies of joy and peace as opposed to the energies of worry and fear. Joy and peace bring strength to our lives. Worry and fear make us feel weak and vulnerable.

When challenges present themselves in your life or when you want to feel stronger and more in tune with your spirit-self, apply the quick fixes. They'll make sure that you get the best out of the day.

Keys to the Abundance

- The quick fixes are a great way to redirect your attention, energy and focus.
- Use them when you need to raise your feelings or boost your energy levels quickly.
- Use them to help reduce stress in your life.

"Emotionally, there are many ways in which you can choose to respond to the difficulties in your life; energetically there are only two ways—positively or negatively . . ."

—*Words from Spirit*

CHAPTER 21

EMBRACING JOY

"As you walk through life remember your joys, touch briefly upon your suffering, look forward to the future and enjoy the present.

This is the best way to keep a healthy mind."

—Words from Spirit

New thinking, new perspectives, new habits—we've been learning how to create these things in relation to joy. To really get the best out of joy, it's important to draw from a foundation of practices that support our newfound thinking. Here are some everyday practices that help us embrace joy to the max!

Welcome Joy

One way to embrace joy is to welcome it into your life. Each day, recite the following affirmation: "I welcome joy to my life. I welcome joy this day!"

Feel good as you recite this uplifting statement, and as you go about your day, look for the evidence of joy unfolding before you.

This affirmation greatly increases our acceptance of joy. Below are some more helpful tips that will enable you to embrace joy more easily.

Respect joy. Know its value and treat it as something that you wish to cultivate in your life. When it's worth something to you, you're more likely to hold it in high regard.

Thrive in joy. Become someone who wants to spread joy, someone who thrives in its energy and wants to improve your life and that of others through joy.

You can achieve this by freely spreading joy to others in ways such as giving gifts, donations, personal time, physical help or kind words, sending uplifting messages to your friends, and even smiling. Mentally, you can help through loving prayers or kind, positive thoughts.

Life will return back to you what you freely give. So when you prosper in joy, joy is returned to you.

Extra tip: Another way to thrive in joy is to leave people feeling better for seeing or speaking to you. When you make it a point to inspire others through your presence and words, you thrive. In raising others, we raise ourselves.

Be thankful for life. Most of us take life for granted. However, life *feels* so much better, and it becomes a far more rewarding experience when we value and appreciate it daily.

To encourage this, revisit the technique of joy-spotting. Say to yourself, "Each day, I will look for something special that occurs." As the day unfolds, discover what that gift is. It may present through the joy of a child's smile, a clear day, or the joy of making someone happy. There are many facets to life that bring great pleasure. Noticing them more often brings happiness to the day.

Express your thanks. When someone does something for you—no matter how small the gesture may be—say *thank you*. When we thank others, we are reminded of the many kind acts that take place in our lives each day. Thank everyone, including those you love and those who serve and help you both inside and outside of your home. It feels good to express thanks.

Be generous. Share or give away things that you do not use. Allow others to benefit from things that you no longer need. Keep the energy of generosity flowing through your life daily. When we are mean-spirited, we block the flow of love and joy into our lives.

You don't have to be financially wealthy to be generous. You can be generous with your prayers and kind thoughts. You can give away excess household goods or clothing in good repair. You can be generous with your time and use it to help others.

Being generous is a great way to keep our joy valve open.

Extra tip: Here is an easy act that spreads joy. Whenever you visit someone, take that person a gift. It can be something as simple as a single flower or a vegetable that you have grown in your garden. You don't have to spend lots of money to be generous at heart. Your intention is what matters—your desire to give—which is an expression of your love.

Give to yourself too. Do things that uplift you. You are deserving of love, and the energy of life *wants you to feel loved*. It's not selfish to care about yourself. Keeping yourself happy and healthy enables you to help others more!

Your enthusiasm for life diminishes when you do not take the time to look after yourself in nourishing ways. So practise the art of self-care and self-love. These practices feed our soul and promote joyful feelings.

Be happy for others. Delight in other people's achievements and successes. When someone tells you some good news, that he or she has received a job promotion, or they have won the lottery, bought a car, a new home, or are about to leave on vacation, be happy for the person! Share in the individual's joy. When you're happy for others, *your* happiness multiplies.

Have fun. Playfulness, laughter, the development of our childlike qualities—all of these things are so important to living our lives in the spirit of joy.

In Summary

Your thoughts and attitudes towards joy count. *You can't fully embrace joy and get the best from it if lurking in the background of your mind are thoughts that undervalue joy.* Establishing thoughts and habits that sanction joy in your life is what transforms your life.

Keys to the Abundance

- Welcome joy into your life. Accept and embrace it with open arms.
- When you respect joy and thrive in it, you transform your life.
- Be happy for others and have fun.

"Feel the love and joy that is within your heart and being. Spread your joy, share it with others. Be a positive light in the lives of others. Lift theirs and your vibrations through the joy that you emanate."

—Words from Spirit

PART V

BRINGING IT ALL TOGETHER WITH THE DAILY CHECKLISTS

The Daily Joy Prayer

Wherever I go, whoever I see, those that I speak of and those who I recall to mind, may all of them, and all beings of life, be filled with love; be uplifted in joy.

Joy to all who inhabit this blessed Earth.

CHAPTER 22

HOW TO START YOUR DAY WITH JOY

"As the day begins, begin your day with positive thoughts. Many of you wake up to the troubles of yesterday; to the worries of the future. Why start your day with occurrences that have passed and thoughts held in time that has not yet occurred?

See a new day as a new start; a fresh morning to which you can think positive, act positive and create a joyful day.

Your first thoughts as you awaken mould your day. Mould your day in a positive way."

—Words from Spirit

Each day is a new start, a fresh beginning, a day where we can make great energy investments. Therefore, it's good to start our days with the best intentions and with positive thoughts.

To help assist you in maximising your daily energy investments, I have created three "joy checklists" that serve as a guide to help you live each day to the full. The checklists will reinforce the best ways you can start, live and end your day with joy.

The checklists tie together all that has been presented in this book.

If you use the checklists every day for a whole month, they will become second nature to you, and you will find that you automatically recall the lists throughout the day.

You can download all three checklists from my website. Enjoy using them, for they are great resources which have the potential to improve your life and remind you that *each day is a gift best lived with joy.*

"How to Start Your Day" Checklist

By improving our thoughts and feelings as we awaken in the morning, we begin the day in a productive way.

Most of us are in the habit of waking up to a mind full of thoughts. For example, we wake up thinking about work-related problems or what we need to do in order to get the children organised or the appointments we must attend during the day. These types of thoughts are not the best ones to begin our day with. They don't maximise our potential, and they don't start our days with good energy investments.

A better way to commence the day is to start it with positive thoughts and feelings. This can be achieved by training our mind to think certain thoughts that are beneficial to our lives and wellbeing. These thoughts and feelings make the best use of our personal energy investments (PEIs).

To begin this mind-awakening training programme, adhere to the following steps:

1. *Begin the day with thanks and appreciation.*

To do this, create a statement in your mind that projects thoughts of appreciation for the day. For example:

- "I give thanks for this day."
- "Thank you for this day and for the gift of life."
- "May my body, mind and spirit be put to good use today."
- "Divine Love, I thank you for this day. I live with unending thanks and gratitude."

Create your own personalised statement (or use one of the listed affirmations) that expresses your appreciation for the day and the gift of life. Once you have given thanks, proceed to the next step.

2. *Welcome joy to your day.*

Mentally create a personalised statement that embraces the energy of joy, one that reinforces the fact that joy is important to you. Here are some ideas:

- "I welcome joy to my life. I welcome joy this day!"
- "Joy, welcome to my day!"
- "Joy, fill my day!"
- "Joy, be a part of my life today."
- "Hooray, I choose to live with joy today!"
- "I love joy. Joy, fill me today."

You can vary your "welcome" statement a little each day if you want to. The key point is that you set the right intentions by *enthusiastically inviting joy* into your life.

Once you have warmly welcomed joy, then there is only one more step to follow, and that is to:

3. Consciously create the day as you want it to happen.

This final step is important because it helps to create your day in a positive way.

Notice the deliberate wording in the third point. It states, "As you **want** it to happen," not "as you don't want it to happen." Avoid creating thoughts where your focus is on what you *don't want*. For example, consider the following thoughts: *I don't want to be late for work today. I don't want to have a stressful day. I don't want the meeting to go badly today. I don't want the kids to drive me nuts. I don't want her to be in a bad mood. I don't want to rush today.*

In all of these examples the focus of your attention is centred on what you don't want!

Remember, energy creates the focus of your attention. It doesn't differentiate between the words *want* and *don't want*. It simply responds to where your attention is mostly held. If you remove the word "don't" from each of the above statements, you will see exactly where your attention is being held! Yikes!

You can easily change these thoughts by thinking and feeling the following:

- "I want to arrive at work on time."
- "I want to have a stress-free day."
- "I want the meeting to go really well today."
- "I want to have a great day with the kids."
- "I want her mood to be lifted."
- "I want the day to unfold smoothly."

This time, your focus is on what you truly want, and energy is attracted to creating these heartfelt desires. You can tell if the statement that you create is worded correctly in two ways. Firstly, as you think and say the statement it will feel positive to you, and secondly, it does not contain the word "don't."

Here are some more examples of statements that focus on how to ask for what you want:

- "I want the problem that has been on my mind to be solved today."
- "I want synchronistic moments to occur in my life today."
- "I want to have a pleasant surprise come my way today!"
- "I want to work efficiently today!"
- "I want more client bookings today."

Think, create, and state clearly *what you want* and then as the day unfolds, look for signs that the things you have asked for are manifesting in your life. Great enjoyment comes from watching how your desires present—usually in the most unexpected and delightful ways.

Keep the requests simple. Do not plan how the outcome will occur. Simply make the statement, "I want such and such a thing to happen," feel positive about it, and then let it go. If you take the request "I want to have a pleasant surprise come my way today" as an example, you will notice that I didn't specify what that surprise must be. I simply asked for something pleasant to occur. In doing this, I allow endless possibilities to manifest and it's amazing what does!

Also ensure that your requests are realistic. You can always check if they are true to you by focusing on your heart. Is what you are asking for resonating with the truth that sits deep in your heart? Does it feel right to you?

Once you have created the day as you want it to be, then finish with a note of gratitude. A simple heartfelt "thank you" to the energy of life is all that is required.

That's it. You can now get on with your day.

When Is the Best Time To Do This?

Ideally, you do the three steps *before* you get out of bed as you become aware of your first thoughts in the morning. It is best to create the thoughts in silence, so make sure that you do not have the radio playing or other distractions going on at the time.

If you forget to recall the steps or perhaps you wake with a start (a crying child, for example), address the situation at hand, and then before you do anything else, you can quietly go through the three steps in your mind.

It can take as little as twenty seconds to do this, and those twenty seconds will be the *best investment you can make for the day.*

And always, as you engage in inner conversation with the energy of life, pay attention to your feelings. Match the right feelings or vibrations with the thoughts that you generate. *Feeling good* about what you are saying and asking for is *essential.*

Where to Place the Checklist

I recommend that you keep the checklist by your bedside so that you have easy access to it. After you have set your intentions and given thanks, then check your checklist to ensure you have covered all of the points.

What Happens if You Forget to Set the Intentions?

If, in reviewing your checklist, you discover that you forgot to include an intention, then simply stop what you are doing, take a moment and set the intention. 'Energy' is not restricted by time, so "the moment" is the perfect time to place your intention.

Checklist

How to Start Your Day with Joy

Today, on awakening, have I:

1. Expressed my thanks and appreciation for this day?
2. Welcomed joy into my life?
3. Set my intentions for a positive day?

Thought for the Day

"Today, I value joy and use joy to improve my day."

"In the dawning of the morn the sounds
of birds call, awakening, arising,
joyfully greeting the new day.

Oh how we encourage all of you to awaken in this
manner, singing, greeting, appreciating the day. You
see the vibrations that you awake to, the spirit in
which you start your day, set the tone for your day.

So Dear Ones, start your day with the
right vibrations. Become aware; and as
the blessing of a new day greets you,
greet it in a blessed and joyful way."

—*Words from Spirit*

CHAPTER 23

HOW TO LIVE YOUR DAY WITH JOY

*"This day join together in the spirit of love; bring
forth your joy; share, be kind, be patient and true.*

*This day live as if it were your last, giving love to
those you love, helping those you wish to help.*

*This day be flexible and accommodating; embrace
change in the spirit of openness and joy.*

*This day laugh as much as you can.
Fill your life, your day with fun.*

*This day live in honour and appreciation
of your life, for this day is a gift that's
why it's called 'the present!'"*

—Words from Spirit

Putting our PEIs to good use can be achieved by focusing on joy as the currency that we transact. When joy is our value of currency, life becomes happier.

For the best investment portfolio that pays high returns, apply the following practices daily:

1. *Live with appreciation.*

Appreciate everything within your day. Learn to appreciate the weather (whatever it is like), the people in your life, your work, your home, the country and city that you live in, and the experiences that grace your day. Be they good, bad, easy or difficult, feel a sense of appreciation for them.

When we appreciate the learning that accompanies tough times, we move through the experiences more easily and effectively. As hard as they are, tough times bring out the best in us, and they make us appreciate good times even more.

As you live your day, live it with appreciation, appreciation and appreciation.

2. *Live with awareness.*

Appreciate yourself in a higher form. Draw on the wisdom of your spirit-self to help you live with more joy. Honour the energy of life and remind yourself that you are in relationship with the energy of life.

Living with awareness drives us to respond to life in less ego-driven ways. It heightens our sense of personal responsibility. We recognise that we need to take charge and improve our actions and responses.

Living with awareness keeps our finger on the pulse of joy. It raises the question, "Are we feeling joy right now?" If not, why not? What has made its presence in our lives less palpable? What tools can we use in order to improve the way that we feel?

3. Use "the tools."

Many tools have been given to you throughout this book, the key ones being the four tools and four factors. Use them to help reduce ego-dominated behaviours and foster joy.

Use the "quick fixes" to help move you out of negative states. Use the "helpful questions" and the various techniques given as pathways to self-empowerment.

Put the tools to work. They are designed to reignite you with the many joyful feelings that are at the heart of your treasure chest, your spirit-self.

4. Do your best.

In all activities that we undertake, we should aim to do our best. This does not mean that we strive to be better than others. It means putting in our best efforts at the time.

When we strive to do our best, we become less focused and opinionated about how others should behave and more focused on our own personal development.

We may not be experts at everything we do, but as long as we do what we do with the best intentions, then we are doing our best.

5. Trust life.

Learn to place your trust in life. Everything that happens is meant to be, including the difficult times that we encounter. Challenging times are a part of life, and they are necessary because they help us grow.

Accepting the unfolding of life helps us to trust life, and trust fosters feelings of contentment and joy.

6. Help someone. Serve with love.

Nothing brings more joy to our being than when we reach out in love to help someone. Extending kindness towards others is one of the main purposes of our lives.

Loving thoughts are an act of service. Our desire to have someone healed; our daily prayers—constitute acts of service. Thoughts of love for others are just as important as the times when we physically or financially help to make someone's life a little easier.

Helping someone will make their day and yours. It's a great way to move out of the worries of your head and into the joy of your heart!

7. Laugh each day.

As important as joy-spotting and as uplifting as dancing is laughter. A day is not well lived if we have not laughed! The energy of joy demands that we loosen up and live life with fun, exuberance and laughter. So make sure laughter is a part of your precious day.

When Is the Best Time to Apply These Practices?

Apply these practices throughout the day and as often as possible. Call to action all that you have learned.

What Happens When We Fail to Apply the Practices?

We all have days when things come unstuck and we forget what we have learned. When this happens, the best way to handle it is to acknowledge that you have gone off track for a while, forgive yourself, and move on.

Do not berate yourself or give up because you fell on old ways. Old habits take time to change. What is important, though, is that you keep trying and applying. In doing so, you will make progress.

Some days we just don't get life right! Acknowledge this, forgive yourself, and march forward.

This checklist will help you to pick yourself up again and give you the right direction in which to march!

Where to Place the Checklist

Post the list in eye-catching places within your home, office or workplace—the fridge, the bathroom mirror, the back of a door that faces your work desk. Alternatively, use the list as a screen saver on your computer.

Checklist

How to Live Your Day with Joy

Today, as I enjoy this day, I will:

1. Live with appreciation.
2. Live with awareness.
3. Use "the tools" to help me.
4. Do my best.
5. Trust life.
6. Serve with love.
7. Have a good laugh.

Thought for the Day

Life is energy. I am energy. Today, through positive thoughts, feelings and actions, I invest my energy wisely.

"Contained within every situation that you encounter is the choice of how you wish to manage that situation. Ultimately the power rests with you in how you wish to respond to the episodes of your life.

Your lifeline of management, your guidance system that will lead you to the most appropriate way to respond is within you—your spirit.

If you choose to be directed by this guidance system your responses will be in harmony with life and for the betterment of your personal development.

Live life wisely. Make your choices in consultation with your spirit."

—Words from Spirit

CHAPTER 24

HOW TO END YOUR DAY WITH JOY

*"Life brings tears, life brings joy. A mixture of
experiences are placed in the melting pot of life.*

*Mixed together they produce a concoction
that many share in the tasting."*

—Words from Spirit

We are never alone. Our life touches others; other lives touch
ours. How interwoven we are. Let's thank all those who come
and go in our life for being a part of our personal story.

I thank you for being a part of mine.

Reflection Time

We have managed the day, and now it's time to reflect on the
day's events by going over the following checklist.

Run through this checklist every night, preferably just before you retire to bed. This practice will reinforce learning. All of the points in the checklist are key points that foster joy.

And as you read the points each night, you'll be surprised at just how many of them you've put into practice and how many you can tick off the list each day!

Where to Place the Checklist

I recommend placing it by your bedside. If you have a prayer room or a place where you meditate before you retire to bed, it is beneficial to keep a copy of the list there. Use the list as a source of daily reflection.

Checklist

How to End Your Day with Joy

Today, did I:

1. Develop eyes of appreciation?
2. Love others?
3. Create positive thoughts and feelings?
4. Live less through my ego-self and more from my spirit-self?
5. Have "time out" for peace?
6. Value and love myself?
7. Serve others?
8. Notice the energy of life's hand at work and did I give thanks for the assistance that came my way?
9. Have a good laugh?
10. Look for something special that occurred?
11. Look for the proof that I co-created in positive ways?
12. Acknowledge abundance in my life?

AND today, when things moved me away from joy, did I use the four tools and four factors to help me?

Four Tools:

1. Examine your thoughts
2. Measure your feelings
3. Now
4. Use your list

Four Factors:

Relationship
Oneness
Love
Energy

You Are Armed!

You are now equipped with many joy-enhancing tools that have the potential to transform your life. As well as the tools, you have three checklists that, when acted on, ensure you make great personal energy investments each day.

I wish you great joy as you travel through the journey of life, and I leave you with a beautiful reminder from *Spirit* of how best to live each precious day.

With love and endless joy,

Helen

"Master the art of happiness. Let the joy of your spirit guide you through the day. Set free the positive energy of your being and feel joy in your demeanor.

Within you happiness abounds. Don't let the layers of life cover over the river of joy that flows through you.

Peel away the layers that bind you. Release the joy. Become a master of your being and allow the real you, the happy you, to shine through. Your life will be uplifted when you do."

—Words from Spirit